BISON
BOOKS

Women in the West

SERIES EDITORS

Sarah J. Deutsch
Duke University

Margaret D. Jacobs
New Mexico State University

Charlene L. Porsild
University of New Mexico

Vicki L. Ruiz
University of California, Irvine

Elliott West
University of Arkansas

Joanne Wilke

Eight Women, Two Model Ts, and the American West

UNIVERSITY OF NEBRASKA PRESS : LINCOLN AND LONDON

A portion of chapter 1 originally appeared as "The Bluffs" in *The Pacific Review* 41, no. 2 (Spring 2002): 20–22.

Portions of chapters 1 and 7 originally appeared as "The Introduction to 'Road Trip 1924': Eight Women, Two Model-Ts, and the American West'" and as "Grandma's Birthday" in *Tributary Magazine* (July 1999 and August 1999, respectively).

A portion of chapter 2 originally appeared as part of an essay titled "Sharing Our Select Fishing Hole" in *The Christian Science Monitor* (May 1988).

Library of Congress Cataloging-in-Publication Data ¶ Wilke, Joanne. ¶ Eight women, two Model Ts, and the American West / Joanne Wilke. ¶ p. cm. — (Women in the west) ¶ ISBN 978-0-8032-6019-1 (pbk. : alk. paper) ¶ 1. West (U.S.)—Description and travel. ¶ 2. West (U.S.)—History, Local. ¶ 3. Young women—Travel—West (U.S.)—History—20th century. ¶ 4. Young women—West (U.S.)—Biography. ¶ 5. Women adventurers—West (U.S.)—Biography. ¶ 6. Women—Iowa—Biography. ¶ 7. Ford Model T automobile. ¶ 8. Automobile travel—West (U.S.)—History—20th century. ¶ 9. Torgrim, Marie Hjelle—Correspondence. ¶ 10. Wilke, Joanne—Family. ¶ I. Title. ¶ F595.w695 2007 ¶ 917.8'033—dc22 ¶ 2007001683 ¶ Designed and set in Minion by R. W. Boeche.

Contents

List of Illustrations   vi

Introduction   1

1. A Beginning   7

2. From Iowa   17

3. We on the Pigmy Road   52

4. Echoes on My Ribs   77

5. From the Cliffs   97

6. Mountain Vistas   112

7. Galloping Bare-Breasted   135

8. A Heap of Living   165

Illustrations

All photographs and identification
courtesy of Marie Hjelle Torgrim

1. All eight women near La Mortle, Iowa
2. Agnes, Laura, Marie, and Grace with Jenny Pep
3. Bess, Christy, Martha, and Zelma with Ophelia Bumps
4. Troublesome spark plugs and Nebraska mud
5. Spark plug experts
6. Bear Creek Canyon
7. On the road from Lookout Mountain
8. Garden of the Gods
9. Early-morning hike up to Bear Lake
10. Bravely lunching in the land of sunshine, sand, and sagebrush
11. Bathing beauties in the Great Salt Lake
12. Sand dunes along the Columbia River Highway
13. Pushing the car up a mountain road
14. A herd of sheep
15. Half Dome, Yosemite National Park
16. Camping grounds at Yosemite National Park
17. The Pacific Ocean
18. Crater Lake National Park
19. At camp in Mount Rainier National Park
20. Mount Rainier National Park, Nisqually Glacier

Eight Women,
Two Model Ts,
and the American West

Introduction

In 1924 eight young women drove across the West in two Model T Fords. They camped out for nine weeks while traveling over nine thousand miles and visiting six national parks—without a man or a gun along. One of these women was my grandmother, another my great-aunt.

I was in my thirties and evaluating my own life when it struck me that their lives were unusual. I set up an interview with my Grandma Marie, her sister Laura, and another traveler named Grace. They were ninety, eighty-five, and eighty-eight respectively. I thought that once they were together their eyes would light up with extraordinary memories; that they would lean forward on their canes and transport me to another time. It didn't happen that way. The trip was no longer a whole to them—they couldn't remember what route they took or which adventure happened where. It was as if vivid vignettes, retold and polished over time, had slipped into their memories as fragments and were now cast in something other than the day-to-day life of driving on dirt roads for nine weeks. It made me think about history, about how subjective it is and how much of it vanishes when anyone dies. It also made me wonder why certain pieces remain.

Grace said, "It all comes back to you in little bits of stories."

Laura told one beautiful tale of park rangers' singing "Rock of Ages" from the bowels of the Carlsbad Caverns as bats flew out in a sky-darkening swarm, but it turned out to be from a different trip. She exclaimed throughout the interview, "I can't believe how much I've forgotten!" She did remember visual scenes—glaciers, lakes, mountains, and colors. Grandma Marie remembered practicalities. She was the leader, responsible for such things. When I asked her what they saw in Yellowstone Park, she answered, "The whole thing." Grace remembered vignettes like the first time she drove or how she felt hiking at altitude without breakfast. Laura commented later that Grace probably remembered so much because she had gone blind. "She's had some time just to sit and think about it."

Other subjects kept popping in—family, mutual friends, current events. The women were so polite it was hard to know what was real. The only disagreement was that Laura loved newspaper comics and Grace thought they were foolish.

When I left the initial interview at Grace's house, Grandma Marie walked behind me and Laura behind her—each one tapping her cane over the buckled sidewalk. "I can't believe how much I've forgotten!" Laura exclaimed again. Grandma Marie's reply was immediate: "That's because you live in the present." This was the main nugget for me from that first interview. The 1924 road trip was just one summer's adventure for these women. It was outstanding only as a beginning.

I tried to piece their hazy memories from 1924 into some semblance of order and time, but there were too many gaps. Surely it was a great, risky adventure that must have thrilled them then, but the giddy rush of facing the unknown didn't hold. Their memories were like dried fruit, innately flavorful and nourishing but without the juice. Still, with an unexpected life of its own their story came to me, often with huge holes and little emotional connection, whether I liked it or not.

Three years after the first interview I discovered Zelma, a fourth living traveler. She gave me the journal she kept, written on the road—complete with a tedious, though precious, listing of every single town they passed through. It was just the framework I needed. But when I asked about the stories—the jokes, the personalities, the arguments— she demurred, saying the others could probably remember those things better. Later she sent me a brief, formal account of the trip she'd written from details in her journal, but I found she sometimes misread her own smudged, penciled hand. For instance, "HOTEL" was underlined in the journal as a single-word description of one of Marie's anecdotes. But in her formal account both her vision and her memory failed, and Zelma wrote that it was "HOT" in Green River, Wyoming.

Two years later Laura died, and her daughter found a trip journal in an upstairs trunk. Laura had kept a running account of her version of the trip, but she apparently forgot that too. Marie died six months after Laura ("It's hard to lose your sister," she said when she was unable to attend the funeral), and two years after that, nearly ten years after the initial interview, a neat bundle of letters appeared on a shelf in the family home. The notation "Mailed home by Marie and Laura on trip to West Coast Summer 1924" was in Marie's handwriting. Obviously the trip was important to her or she wouldn't have taken the time. Still, she compiled these letters, titled and stored them carefully, then forgot them.

As my feelings for the ladies and my sense of the spirit of the story evolved, my frustrations mounted. I believed their 1924 summer trip was interesting, unusual, and a history worth telling, but there was so much more to these women than that. Laura and Grandma Marie had a powerful impact on my life. I experienced their strength, their zest for living, and a simultaneous connection to and dissonance with each other. But in the modest way of their generation, their stories depicted little of this—little of themselves—and I only knew them as old.

I looked at the old photographs, taken on their trip with a Brownie box camera. Some are sharp and some are not—a reminder that in those days Kodak processed the film but did not make the prints. This step was done at home. Someone, most likely Grandma Marie, laid the negative right on the paper, exposed it to light, and soaked it in chemicals to develop and fix it. Not a very precise method, especially without benefit of photo equipment or indoor plumbing.

The album pages are black construction paper, and each of the fifty-nine pictures is captioned in white ink in Grandma Marie's handwriting. There she is as a young woman swimming in the Great Salt Lake ("got a swig up my nose that nearly knocked me out"), and there is her sister, Great-Aunt Laura, grinning while pushing a Model T ("mountain roads"). Here they are wading in the Pacific Ocean ("great sport to have the surf rush up"), sliding down a glacier on Mount Rainier ("snow in July"), and standing beside their Model T Ford ("the whole gang"). They are sturdy girls, with bobbed hair and wearing knickers. I could almost hear Grandma Marie chuckle as she looks over the pictures with me. "There weren't slacks for women then," she said, "so we had to wear knickers." What else was lacking for women who wanted to drive across the West in 1924?

Tucked in the back of the photo album is a modern portrait of Marie and Laura. My husband took it at the last family reunion they presided over. It was the first year that beer came out from behind the corncrib and cold ham sandwiches weren't served at lunch. Laura is eighty-seven and Marie ninety-three, two white-haired old women in flower-print dresses. Marie leans on the silver handle of her cane and looks straight into the camera without hesitation, her skin still soft and beautiful. Laura gazes up and away, admiring the beauty of the trees, her lips parted. How could I do them justice?

I wrote other stories about Grandma Marie and Laura as I knew them, about other generations in our family, and about myself. The connection I sought was elusive, but as I washed my own experiences and emotions together with theirs a certain sensibility crept into me. Although separated by time, age, and geography, I found our stories blended so naturally that it should have been obvious: although the juice of their stories had evaporated long ago, I still wore the scent. To evoke their youthful selves, I had to remember mine.

1. A Beginning

I first saw the bluffs when I was four. We drove from California to Iowa in a Volkswagen Bug. I could stretch out in the back seat, with my little sister in the space behind that we called the back window. It was the first of many car trips to Iowa, always in the summer. The July heat was miserable, with little fluctuation day or night. Who wanted to visit Iowa when it was ninety degrees or more with 90 percent humidity? Or drive across Nevada or Nebraska without air-conditioning? Even Mom doesn't understand it anymore; she says she wanted to show off her little family. But every year? Our record was forty-two hours straight. At least at night the sun wasn't beating on you through the windows. Once at the farm, we unstuck our thighs from the vinyl upholstery, tumbled from the car like overcooked spaghetti, and staggered bleary-eyed toward the bathroom. At least we could move.

Grandma Marie and Grandpa met us in the gravel driveway, under the towering elm tree, oblivious to our stale odor. They lived in a white frame house on top of a hill, bordered with hollyhocks. Around and behind it were arranged the corncrib, chicken house, garage (which was the original home), old outhouse, and huge red barn, with various wooden and wire fences and a concrete watering trough big enough for swimming but too filthy. In the distant fields we could hear the lowing of black-and-white cattle and the chugging of old tractors.

By the next day we kids were clean and rested and into it all. The old frame house and farm were novelties for us, raised in single-level California homes. Instead of playing on manicured squares of lawn, we raced barefoot across a yard of mowed weeds, treacherous with thistles, and screamed across endless wild pastures.

Grandma Marie always arranged a family gathering, but not at her home. We drove a mile into the sweltering, breathless lowlands to the family home, the Brick House by the bluffs. In California we had only two cousins, and most of our socializing was with friends we chose. In Iowa it was a multigenerational swarm of relatives. Perhaps Mom had an inkling of the texture available there, and that was what fueled our journeys, or maybe she craved the familiarity of these gatherings.

Once the meal was over, the youngsters weren't expected to sit still and be polite. The heat and mosquitoes at the Brick House were the worst, but the lightning bugs in the evening and the frogs, fish, and coolness along the trout spring drew us away from chatting adults. We ran as a pack, hunting arrowheads above the spring, searching out half-wild kittens in the barn, and shouting as we swung and leaped from ropes in the hayloft. We roamed the hills and climbed the bluffs, white limestone cliffs rising straight from the yard. Hiking to the tip of the Big Bluff was a rite of passage, both the first time you were taken up and the first time you climbed it alone.

My great-grandfather, Grandma Marie's father, bought the bluffs instead of bottomland because they reminded him of Norway, his homeland. It was an impractically romantic choice in the northeastern corner of Iowa, where farms are judged by the amount of tillable ground among the rolling hills and limestone outcroppings. His children grew up there. In spring when the oak buds reached the size of a mouse's ear, they discarded their shoes and ran through the lush green up, up into the woods, and the hillsides embraced them. More than the house, these cliffs defined their home.

On that first trip to Iowa when I was four, Uncle Bill and Aunt Darlene and their five kids were already at the Brick House when we arrived. My cousin Renee was five. "We climbed the bluffs yesterday," she said. I remember looking up at the mottled white cliffs. With no perception of distance, I thought they were farther away and taller, and I imagined my cousins as small as ants climbing straight up the craggy face. "My brother jumped from one to the other," she continued. I couldn't picture that at all.

The next morning Renee whispered, "I'll take you up the bluffs, but don't tell anyone." We hovered at the back screen door, looking out for the rooster and his flashing spurs. It took only a moment to learn to fear him, longer to learn to carry sticks to defend ourselves. We made a dash for the woodshed and crept through the nettles along the back until we could peer around and run for the corncrib, then duck under the electric fence and slip down a short bank into the dry creek bed and safety.

The creek bed was white with limestone, the rocks dry and light as old bones and covered with fossils. Back then this creek still flooded every spring, washing away last year's growth and debris and uncovering new rock faces. We were supposed to follow the creek up a ways and then turn onto a steep cow path up the back end of the bluffs, but Renee was losing her nerve. She couldn't remember the right trail. Finally we turned around. We were chased by the rooster and stung by wasps on the way back.

That afternoon Uncle Bill took a bunch of us up. How he knew the right cow trail we couldn't figure. It led to the wooded portion of the ridge. From there we hiked on level ground, glimpsing space through the trees. The trail ended abruptly with a crack in the earth. The rocky point split away from the lush underbrush, and we peered from the safety of the trees as if from a cave. Though the chasm separating us from the limestone tip was only a foot wide, it was twenty feet deep. My head spun and I felt as if it could suck me right down, but I held Uncle Bill's hand and leaped across. Renee crawled around.

You can see a long way from the tip of the Big Bluff, but there isn't much to see—cornfields, farmhouses, and roll-ing, tree-covered hills vanish into the humid haze. The bluffs themselves are the most beautiful things around. A flock of pigeons flew by, wheeling together, the sound of wind on feathers changing with every turn. I wondered what it would be like to jump off. We waved at our moms and the babies down below and hiked back. I told my sister I had jumped from one bluff to the other. She squinted up in disbelief as I tried to point out where.

Three years later my mom took my sister and me up. I was surprised by her sudden competence and confidence in these woods. Though she'd lived in Albuquerque, Seattle, and Los Angeles, my mother's first response to something new was al-ways the startled resistance of the fourteen-year-old country kid named Gertrude.

Looking back I realize it was a new experience for me, not her. I'd never put my foot on a strand of barbed wire and lifted the higher strand to let someone through. I didn't know where the gates were and couldn't tell one manure-stained cow trail from another. That winding mesh of pathways was to me what the Los Angeles freeways must have been to her. She grew up running over these hills, learning the lay of the land the same way she taught herself to read. She grew up on a nearby farm, on the edge of the prairie, but whenever the extended family gathered at the Brick House on Sundays and holidays, she came here and explored it all.

On the way back she took us on a different trail. It curved from the middle of the ridge out to the lip of the cliff and through a small clearing. My mother said that Great-Uncle Ben had killed a wolf there with an ax while the family watched from below. Then the trail cut sharply down a rocky cleft and ended when our feet sank into leaves. The light changed from glaring to cool beneath the canopy of trees, and the hillside below us was still nearly vertical with little underbrush, only tree trunks. As if through a curved tunnel, we could see the Brick House below.

Mom said, "What you do is pick a close tree and run for it." We watched in horror as she demonstrated. This was not our mother. But we found it was truly more dangerous to try going slow than to simply fling ourselves forward through the ankle-deep leaves. So we hurled ourselves from tree to tree, screaming toward the bottom.

One day many years earlier my grandmother, a young Marie, stood on the tip of the Big Bluff and watched ash pour into the sky on a high wind, dimming the sun. Soot and the smell of smoke carried from the 1910 forest fires on the western boundary of Montana all the way to eastern Iowa. Marie, at age twelve, imagined her brother Sig in a spray of sparks, skin smeared black, as he fought a wall of flame with a shovel. She could practically smell his singed hair as she watched the sunset over her pastoral view turn to blood.

Marie's six older brothers all went west; it was practically expected of them. They built roads, bridges, and railroads and worked on timber crews, in mining camps, and in oil fields. Herman, who graduated from grade school with her, never went to high school. Instead he springboarded across the West from brother to older brother, traveling from North Dakota to Montana, Canada, and ultimately Washington, working as a laborer. Marie saw her brothers come home changed, as if by looking out across the grand vistas of the West they realized they could see beyond their noses. She wanted that for herself.

Over time, with years of leaning on the neighbors' fence and gazing toward the horizon, Marie developed a plan. First she needed money. "Back in those days," she remembered, "there were only two professions for women, to be a teacher or a nurse. I had no desire to be a nurse, and so I had to be a teacher." After high-school graduation and a few years of rural teaching, she attended "teachers college" (now the University of Northern Iowa) in Cedar Falls, Iowa, to earn her teaching certificate and be eligible for better-paying jobs.

"[It was] not a university," she remembered; "I guess the university was fancier. The teachers college was . . . kind of looked down upon. But [it was important]; they only had one in the state."

"We had to live on a shoestring," she continued, "I remember that one house where Laura and I stayed to start with.

We had our rooms upstairs, and we cooked and ate down in the basement. That wasn't a very nice place down there, and Laura never gets tired of telling [how] when she came downstairs to cook . . . there was a rat sitting in the frying pan. That rat, her college, that's what she remembers. That's the kind of style we had."

Later, after graduation, Marie accepted a job at the teachers college, where she taught young girls how to teach, helping them earn their valued certificates. She earned the required master's degree from Columbia University in New York during summer breaks. "It was expensive to be in New York," Marie remembered, "awful expensive." But she couldn't teach at Cedar Falls without her master's degree.

Still, her original goal never wavered. "I wanted to see Yosemite," Marie said simply. "And back then driving and camping was the cheapest way to travel." She was sure she could find three others to fill the car, and from Iowa, Estes Park was on the way to Yosemite, as were Pikes Peak and the Great Salt Lake. A Model T cost just over $500, including license, and she could pay over time at thirty-two dollars a month. Fifty dollars worth of gear and two months of car payments split between four travelers wouldn't be much, and she'd heard they could sell the car for a profit in California to pay for the train ride home.

Or—and her hands tingled at the thought—they could make a big loop and see Crater Lake, Mount Rainier, and Yellowstone on the way home. Her brother Herman was in Montana then, and brothers Ole, Ben, and Carl were in North Dakota. She traced the maps with her fingers, adding up mileage in her head: nine thousand miles.

When Marie mentioned a trip to Yosemite, her friends Agnes and Grace at once agreed to go. It was the 1920s: things were booming, the world was changing, and life was full of excitement. Almost overnight the bobbed-haired flapper, drinking liquor and dancing to wild music, replaced the image of the old-fashioned, useful maiden aunt, a bastion of American family life. Although for some it was a time of excess, Marie remembered that they were country kids, taught to be decent and hardworking. Perhaps her personal life did not encompass the extravagance of new morality, bootlegging, and all the stereotypes, but the essence of the Roaring Twenties trickled down everywhere, even to Iowa. People took to the new sense of freedom and took to their cars. The Model T, part durable wagon and part modern technology, was a breakthrough allowing hordes to venture out, to venture west, whether roads were available or not.

Agnes and Grace both grew up near Marie, and like her were recent graduates from teachers college. "Agnes was good at a lot of things," Marie noted, "and was used to driving." Grace was quiet and bright, had a farm girl's good sense, and was already working at a better-paying job with her graduation certificate. Marie asked her sister Emma to come, but she didn't have any money. She had not yet finished college, and though teaching at a distant country school, Marie noted, "she was having a good time and spending [all] her money." But their youngest sister, Laura, was ready to go. Only nineteen years old, she had taught two seasons at their own rural school and had saved her money. Laura remembered that she was happy teaching at the country school and driving the team in the fields for her brother Walter—until Marie brought up this trip.

Marie was pleased with the group; she believed they were all competent and could get along well for two months in tight quarters. Still, everyone agreed that bringing a second car would be safer, because then one could always rescue the other. "We just rattled our brains to find four other girls who would take this trip," Marie remembered, "The other car was kind of a conglomeration of people from here and there."

Christy was from Marie's high-school class. The other three were generally referred to together, like a gaggle of poultry. Bess was a friend of Agnes, but no one was really sure how the other two were invited—friends of friends or classroom acquaintances from teachers college. Marie described Zelma as not very confident and said, "Martha came from people who couldn't think fast."

In an interview Marie remembered what a "hard time we had to get permission from our folks to take the trip. They thought we would all be killed."

> Well, the two of us wanted to go. My mother and
> father thought . . . we'd never come back. I remem-
> ber I argued with them and told them there was
> no danger . . . but it didn't do any good. Finally I
> said to them, "Now," and then I named a couple
> of people in my high-school class that were pretty
> wild, they were running around and doing things
> that were kind of shady. So I said, "We live decent
> lives; you never hear anybody saying those things
> about us, and then when we want to do some-
> thing decent and learn something, then you won't
> let us do it." That was the argument I had, and
> they finally gave in to that.

Marie was twenty-six years old at the time. She found out later that Grace just announced to her parents that she was going. Then Marie bought one car and Zelma bought the other, and they made plans to meet in Marshalltown, Iowa.

"June 12, 1924; Left home at 6:00," Laura wrote in her journal. "I bawled." How else could she describe it? The Model T sat by the woodshed, with a narrow cupboard bolted to the passenger side, canvas side tent and cots lashed to the running board, her drawing pad on the passenger seat. She'd never left home before.

I imagine a flurry of jokes with the family and quick hugs, soft, wet, and whiskered cheeks. Laura cranks the motor to gassy life, her sister Marie behind the wheel. Their stout mother waves from the steps until they are out of sight, connected to them by the reddened tips of her fingers. Laura remembers her recent buggy ride to Conniver, in the next county. Ten miles each way, and it was a long trip. Now they planned to drive hundreds of miles and be gone for weeks.

They bump over the narrow homemade bridge and down the maple-lined lane and turn west. Laura watches the bluffs recede and clutches her drawing pad to quiet her shaking hands.

2. From Iowa

When I say "Iowa saved me," my friends ask "From what?" I could say from the modern world, but it really wasn't a matter of being rescued from stormy family seas or moving from one life into another. Rather, like my grandparents' farm home, my life in Iowa encompassed dim attics and musty basements that I sensed, imagined, explored, and hid in. Going to Iowa added a texture and dimension to my life and my imagination that simply wasn't available in a single-level single-family home in the California suburbs. It was as if a creative switch was thrown for me in the recesses of that house, and my pupils dilated.

When I was ten I took an airplane from San Francisco to Minneapolis, the major airport closest to my grandparents' farm. It was my first trip alone. Later it became an annual event, with family either dropping me off or picking me up, and me spending at least a month on the farm with my grandparents. It was just what my family did. Young cousins often traveled to visit each other. In 1924 Marie's oldest nephew, John, spent the summer with his grandparents at the Brick House. We are a family of teachers. Expanding children's horizons comes naturally.

My first solo plane trip had a two-hour layover in Denver. "Stay on the plane," my mother admonished for two weeks beforehand, all the way to the airport, with her red nose warning of tears, jabbing her finger for emphasis. I did. It seemed like a simple enough thing to me. I sat with another girl in the very last seat. She had a blanket over her knees and magazines to look at and seemed so mature and self-possessed. I was glad when she got off in Denver and I went on alone. Miles high and far from the regular adults, a spirit of adventure began to creep over me.

In Minneapolis I walked from the stale, cool, dry air of the plane into earth-scented humidity. I sucked in the scent, filled with richness, heat, and moisture. I didn't pause before descending the narrow steps to the hot runway, but that moment of emerging, of entering "Iowa" on my own for the first time, seems longer in my memory than a few quick steps. At the time only the air was different.

Life with my grandparents revolved around family. Several of Grandma Marie's siblings (my great-aunts and great-uncles) still lived in the area and took any excuse to gather at the Brick House for casseroles, Jell-O salad, and sweet corn. They enjoyed visiting the place as much as the people. Laura and Vic, Albert and Alice, Herman and Ilene, the bachelor brother Walter, and my grandparents and me gathered regularly for potlucks, fishing trips, sweet-corn freezing parties, and fiftieth wedding anniversaries. I was the little towhead in the middle of all those grandmothers and grandfathers, the quiet one who listened to everything they said.

Uncle Herman was very deaf. He couldn't understand all the inside talk, so he sat by himself in the yard, completely comfortable in his silence and the scenery. It seemed natural to follow him, and he told me memories, like the time he tied his hysterical wife to a tree with his belt before jumping into a river to save their young son. His wide face and nose and long ears reminded me of a badger. He taught me how to hug a gate open and closed and how to tie a bowline, though I could never get it snug against the horses' necks the way he did with those coarse laborer's fingers.

Aunt Laura taught me rosemaling, a form of Norwegian folk painting. She watched my brushstrokes with an expression I didn't recognize. "It's there in your hands, isn't it?" she said. Uncle Albert showed me how to tell if sweet corn was ripe just by squeezing it. "It has to be firm with a little squish to it. If you tear it open and it isn't ripe, the birds will get it." Uncle Walter lived alone in the kitchen at the Brick House, the family home where we gathered. His bed, a sheetless mattress on a creaky metal frame, blocked the door leading to the rest of the run-down house. He wasn't much of a farmer— he couldn't stand destroying the birds' nests by mowing hay. An orphaned kitten lived behind his fridge, and his dog slept over the pilot light in the oven.

At every gathering they told stories—about themselves, about each other, about how the farm used to be—and I inhaled them along with the smell of rural humidity, old leather, coffee, and Walter's cigar smoke, as if into my own cells. For a long time I thought everyone knew these reminiscences. I'm still amazed each time I relate a detail that no one else in the family knows. But more than their stories, it was experiencing these people who grew up close to the land, a generation born at the turn of the twentieth century. The way they lived and worked and related to each other and to me, and their humor, was as important as the words they spoke.

Grandma Marie talked to me the most, just the two of us sitting at the kitchen table, her swollen, arthritic finger caressing the red-and-white oilcloth as she spoke. Her face was round, with soft old skin that stayed beautiful, her hair a coarse-looking mixture of original brown and aging gray and white, cut by my grandfather in some ongoing imitation of a bob. She had a flap of skin near her left eye that we called her little nose and the pale necklace of a scar curving around the base of her throat where her thyroid was removed.

I remember that face looking down at me through dark-rimmed cat's-eye glasses—a stern teacher's face. I was four years old and crying because Brownie, her beloved greyhound, had just bitten me. But instead of enveloping my shock, outrage, and pain in a soft grandmotherly hug, she asked, "Why did Brownie bite you?"

"Because I was trying to ride her," I replied through my sobs, imagining a dog as tall as a horse and holding up my injured finger that wasn't quite bleeding.

"I bet you won't do that again," she said. It wasn't at all what I expected.

I read recently that there are no grandmother stories in our culture—no wisdom passed from old women to younger ones. My Grandma Marie didn't offer wisdom either, at least not directly. She offered herself.

She told me about growing up on the farm and attending the one-room school at the end of the lane where she later began her teaching career, about saving what she earned to help finance her own and her sisters' college educations or to travel.

She told me about my real grandmother, her sister Emma. When Emma wanted a closet and Grandpa put her off too long, she smashed a hole in the wall with an ax. When a bull gored Emma's father-in-law, she rescued him with a pitchfork. When Emma died leaving three young children and a family ripped apart, Grandma Marie stepped in to help. She and my grandfather fell in love and married, and I grew up with a mythic grandmother along with the flesh-and-blood one.

Grandma Marie told me about her life and travels, but not as if they were outstanding or unusual. Yes, she and seven other women drove two Model T Fords from Iowa to the West Coast and back in 1924. They visited Yosemite, Crater Lake, Mount Rainier, and Yellowstone. Yes, she took a ship to Norway in 1928 and toured Europe by train. She bought a dress in Paris because she thought she should and sat at the captain's table on the way home from England—but that was because he was taken with her sister Laura. Yes, she got dysentery in Mexico in the '30s, and though "it was no fun at the time," when she lived in Egypt for three years after World War II she was immune and was the only American who could eat and drink in local people's homes and thus become more intimate with them.

She toured the pyramids while she was in Egypt, learned to dislike camels, and saw ancient artifacts just sticking out of the sand. But mostly she talked about the poverty there, pained that it still existed. She went to help establish a teachers school and a library so the people could educate and improve themselves. On the train from Cairo she saw people sitting against a wall in the dust, their eyes black. At every town they passed through she peered out the grimy train windows and saw more, sitting so still she wondered if they were alive, their eyes black holes. When at last she climbed from the train into the blaring heat, she realized the blackness was flies. The people were too weak and tired to brush them from their eyes.

The image of Grandma Marie walking out to her garden with her wicker basket and hoe is permanent in my memory. Her thin brown calves bow up from earth-colored shoes and ankle socks into a long, square cotton skirt, and her white blouse is untucked. She always came home with her basket full of tomatoes, bell peppers, corn, or potatoes. I remember her sitting at the kitchen table going over a cake pan filled with ripe raspberries, picking out the stems and leaves. She pointed at the window screen, which was alive with a thick mat of insects. "They followed me," she laughed. "Wouldn't they like to get in here!"

Once when I was four she came back to the house with her basket full of pea pods. She sat in a metal lawn chair in the shade and invited all the cousins to help her shell them. The others were quickly bored and melted away to the tire swing or the corncrib, but I liked popping the fat pods open and freeing the crisp green balls. I loved watching our bowl fill, from a handful of peas that thunked against the ceramic to brimming green. Each little pod added and added on, until we had enough peas to feed everyone.

Marie, Laura, and Grace arrived at Zelma's family home in Marshalltown, Iowa, to find tents, cots, bedrolls, dishes, food staples, fishing gear (including worms), chains, tire pump, folding luggage carriers, and everyone's luggage strewn across the yard, with the Model T in the middle. They weren't even packed yet, and all that luggage!

It turned out the other girls had spent the morning learning how to drive. The salesman showed Zelma how when she bought the car, and she taught the others. Grace later commented on their limited driving experience. She had learned to drive three days before they left for California. "I was dating . . . ," she began, then corrected herself, "I happened to meet a young [sales]man and I told him my plight: I didn't know how to drive. He said, 'I'll take you out.' So we had three days, and he took me out on the highway . . . and showed me what I needed to know about driving a Ford. Three days . . . that was the end of my driving experience. So we did something very foolish."

Laura was introduced to everyone. Zelma was called sarcastically by her last name, Silence, though her nickname was Boob. Martha was petite, pixyish, and Catholic. And Bess was also smaller than the Norwegian country girls, with billowing dark hair and a generous smile.

Zelma insisted that they tour Marshalltown before lunch, and Laura wrote in her journal, "Agnes acted [as] chauffeur around Marshalltown. [Zelma's brother] John contracted serious illness and couldn't go to work."

After the tour, they set to work loading the Fords. In interior space a Model T roughly compares to a Volkswagen Bug, but still they fit four people, luggage, camping gear, and even food into each one. Packing everything in and onto the cars was like a puzzle. They eyed the sizes and shapes, comparing every item to the various cubbies.

Gradually everything was sorted out. The stove leaked gas and they abandoned it, along with some of the cookware. They rolled cots and bedding inside canvas tents and lashed them to the back fenders. They attached flexible luggage racks to the full length of the driver's-side running board (there was no driver's door anyway) and filled them with suitcases, chairs, and Zelma's car bed. They stored food and cooking utensils in the cupboards, whose hinged covers folded down into tables. A canvas bag filled with water for the radiator hung from the side.

Zelma later wrote, "We were much like Courtney Ryley Cooper, when in *High Country* he says, 'I carry everything from stove to dish pan to say nothing of a broiler, six of everything for eating, frying pan, stew pot and coffee pot. It weighs less than 12 pounds. It took a bit of shopping but it was found.' We spent $36 for equipment before we started, but sold it for $20 to a second-hand man when we returned."

They didn't get started until midafternoon. Later Zelma wrote, "We stopped at sister Leola's near La Mortle, Iowa, to get some oats to pack our eggs in." Marie remembered her Brownie box camera while there and, amid a flurry of combs, asked Leola to take their picture. "Marie had a camera before anybody else around had a camera," Laura noted. Marie remembered that it was "a little box camera. They were the cheapest you could buy. They took very good pictures . . . nice and clear."

To get the full length of both cars Leola walked out into a plowed field. In the picture eight blurry girls in knickers stand between two loaded cars with tall spoked tires, their faces so smudged and small they can be identified only by their various hats. The other half of the picture is clear and sharp: row upon row of turned sod. Marie labeled the photo "the whole gang."

"By that time it was the middle of the afternoon," Zelma noted, "and we decided to go no further than Ames, where we knew there was a good campground to spend the first night. We could try out our gear, and if we had forgotten anything we could return."

"In those days," Marie remembered, "They didn't have the motels like now, so every town had a campground and wood ready for making a fire. Some had showers or gas stoves. You never knew just what you might encounter, but on the edge of every town there was a campground."

Once in camp, they lashed side tents to the tops of the cars and drove stakes into the ground to hold them. They set up two cots inside each tent. "Our tent was easy to erect," Zelma noted. "There were not poles or wooden stakes, but only a couple of ropes and sharp steel stakes for the places where one hits rocks a few inches below the ground surface."

I imagine the girls in Zelma's car, dubbed "Ophelia Bumps," installed their car bed, which fit over the front and back seats. Marie saved that expense by having the front seats in her car, "Jenny Pep," cut and hinged so they simply folded back. The bed was not flat, no matter how they stuffed it with newspapers, coats, and pillows. They called it their "marcelled bed" after the wavy hairstyle.

Laura wrote home, "Marie and Grace are the cooks in our car. Ag and I pitch tent and make beds; the result is that *we* are very comfortable."

Zelma wrote, "Nobody could stop us!"

Ames, Iowa
June 13, '24

Dear Folks,

Well, we have pitched camp, had our supper and will soon retire. Fine moonlite nite and nice tourist camp here. We started from Gladbrook about 7:00 this morning and got into Marshalltown about 8:30. Had a lot to do to get the two cars all fixed, so we didn't get started from there till about 3:00 p.m. Came to Ames—about 35 mi. We drove up around the college—beautiful grounds. We are starting for Omaha in the morning. Grace, Martha, Christine and I are on as the first shift of cooks. The others pitch the tents and make beds. There are quite a few tourists in this camp tonight. Laura has gone to bed.

Marie

The next morning it was raining as they repacked, lashing, stuffing, and squeezing everything in and on those little cars. "We were not much different than others who start on a camping trip with everything but the kitchen sink," wrote Zelma. "The gross weight was never considered, [or] that we ourselves weighed anything." Horses would be given some care, but people weren't used to traveling by motorcar. A twenty-horsepower machine seemed indomitable. Zelma remembered passing "tourists" with cars packed so full of folding chairs and mattresses that they had to ride with their feet sticking out the windows.

They discussed buying enough bread for the whole trip. Marie remembered this discussion as an example of their inexperience. It would have been stale within days. Then they decided that each day one person in each car would be responsible for all the driving. "You might have fifty miles or you might have three hundred," Grace said, "but it was your day to drive." They figured it would all even out in the end. Then they sat down with a map and chose a destination for the day. "We weren't very scientific about it," Marie noted. "Just so many miles because . . . those Fords didn't go very fast and there weren't any decent roads. So [we] just rambled along."

When they left Ames, it was Grace's day to drive. She remembered, "It rained and it rained and it rained, and I thought 'Oh, you!'" Laura and Marie had different accounts of the weather that day. Marie wrote home, "We drove along with no happenings until we got to Carroll. There it rained a little. We put on side curtains, and as the roads were graveled and it soon passed over, we drove on. The farther west we came we could see it had rained quite a bit. The roads were good, however, so we drove right along without needing chains." But Laura's addition to the same letter noted, "The roads were quite bad as a creek had overflowed its banks and flooded the road in several places. It really wasn't bad for Agnes and me, as we only drive from the rear (Here you were s'posed to laugh)."

Later Laura wrote in her journal, "Country flat. Large corn fields," as the familiar rolling hills of home gave way to straightaways and an unchanging view of fields and fields and more green fields. "Ralston, Glidden, Carroll, rain, Westside, Vail, stuck in mud," Zelma wrote in her journal. Each little town was very much like the last, with its crossroads and post office, and they passed through every muddy one. At Boone they bought some chalk and wrote "Ophelia" and "Jenny Pep" on their cars. Zelma remembered, "The others called their car Jenny Pep when she ran well and plain Jenny when she didn't." In Stanton they added "California or Bust."

Zelma noted, "We decided if our cars were ever separated, the lead car would wait at the post office (every town has one)." Marie remembered, "There was no way to get communication."

They drove through the gray wet, the lightweight cars battered by sheets of rain. Model Ts are not enclosed vehicles but "touring cars" open on the sides, with a glass windshield split into top and bottom and a treated canvas top (called rubber covering). Oiled canvas "side curtains" were put up over the windows for wind, rain, and cold (there were no heaters) and were held in place with rods that fit into the doors and twisting button snaps around the perimeter. Even when the curtains were buttoned snugly, corners still flapped and sometimes blew loose. Marie remembered, "We had to carry those curtains under the seat, then when it rained you had to . . . get those curtains up . . . so it didn't rain on you." "Isinglass" peepholes in the curtains allowed limited visibility. (Isinglass was made of thin sheets of crackled mica.) There were no windshield wipers, but since they couldn't go very fast the sloping roof generally protected enough of the windshield to let them see. Other, damper options included folding up the top portion of the windshield or sticking your head out the window.

The sky was dark to the south, warning of hail and tornadoes, and the dirt highways sopped up the downpour, quickly turning from thin, muddy bisque to the sucking thick pudding called "gumbo" that Iowa was known for. Although the Salt Lake desert was the most feared and most dangerous stretch of the highway west, Iowa gumbo probably accounted for the most difficulty and delay. There were mud holes with names, notorious spots where parallel tracks led through the ditch and around thigh-deep wallows. Years later, after tractors became common but before the country roads were graveled, farmers took to parking their tractors near these holes. They tied a stout rope to the back and left the key in the ignition, so travelers could pull themselves out. In 1924 you just had to push.

"A car just went by and told us we'd get into mud a foot deep," Laura wrote in a letter to Emma. "That's what we can bank on, as he showed us with his paws that it was about three feet, but [he] got through with a low-hanging car." In her journal she added, "Near Denison [Christy] got stuck, pulled out by tourists." Marie elaborated: "[Christy] has never driven a Ford but is learning fast. Think she will be good, as she's cool and nervy and the others get rather rattled."

As the day progressed, they put on chains and waited for each other at the mud holes, adding cars to the train as they went. The cars slithered and slipped around weeping chuckholes, bogging and heaving through heavier mud that engulfed the tires, hiding the spokes. Later on this heavy baggage dried on the wheels, compressed, then flew off in pie-shaped wedges, littering the highway.

"When we came into Denison," Marie wrote, "the others . . . had picked up a couple of [hitch]hikers from Linn, Mass. Can't see what possessed them to load their flivver like that. One of [the hikers] was driving—maybe they did it to get a chauffeur."

In the afternoon Grace started down a hill and saw "a great lot of water down there." A creek had flooded the road at the bottom. "Instead of slowing down, I put on the gas," she said. "I was afraid we'd get stuck if I didn't. You should have heard the screams!"

I imagine their frail-looking car flying down a mud-slick hill and into the pool of flooded gumbo below. A wave of mud splashes over them, popping side curtains and dousing everything with slime. Jenny Pep shimmies and fishtails, farting in discontent, her narrow tires spinning. Amid the screams and the splattering, Grace holds tight to the wheel, her fingers pushing hard on the throttle and spark, until at last Jenny heaves out the other side, coughs, and dies. Grace was proud of herself, despite disagreement with her method.

They took turns climbing out to throw the crank, but Jenny wouldn't fire. Soon Ophelia arrived with her two hitchhikers, who showed them how to clean and dry their timer, which sat at the bottom of the motor.

They stopped at the Council Bluffs campground, overlooking the flooded Missouri River. "Grace drove . . . yesterday and did very well—she does as well as the rest of us," Marie noted in a letter home.

> We got in here about 8:30. Those [hitchhikers] left then. Guess they were perfectly respectable, but we decided to not pick up any more, as it isn't playing safe. Grace and I were taking our showers when [the rain] started. It rained so hard that Grace and I didn't go back to the car for some time. The wind blew fierce and we were worried about the rest. Could see the tents though, and saw they stayed up OK. Laura and Agnes hadn't been a bit scared as they were hi and dry, although there was quite a bit of water on the ground. If we'd been in a low place instead of on a hill, we'd been out of luck, I'm afraid.

Laura wrote, "Agnes was draping herself gracefully on her cot when she became aware of a flood on our floor—Agnes pulled her feet up."

In the middle of the night another storm came in, with tremendous lightning and thunder and wind. Marie wrote, "Laura and I were entirely dry in the car. A little water came thru the tent, and no wonder as it beat down so hard." Zelma noted, "We fastened the side curtains as much for rain as for protection from peeping toms. We heard the thunder and saw the lightning, but the funniest sight when we peeped out was the man [in the next campsite]. The wind blew and the lightning showed him holding the center pole of his tent while the tent and his nightshirt flapped around his bare legs!"

They woke to another gray sky, and their spirits hung as limp and damp as their clothes. They pulled up stakes and shook off the tents as they once again began to stuff those little cars. But Marie wouldn't have it. Marie was the eldest, Grace remembered. "She seemed to have the patience and wisdom, and knew what to say and do." Marie thought there was too much luggage. She and Laura shared one bag between them, and she felt the others could too. "We had to be very careful about what we [took]," Marie said in interview, "I made them go through their suitcases to be sure they needed all that. If they didn't, they had to take it out, because those Fords couldn't have a very heavy load."

Zelma wrote, "We reduced to two [bags per] car by packing only one dress for each along with seldom-used garments in one. In the other were towels, PJs (flannel for cold nights) and other things used daily." They shipped the rest home and set out in the rain.

> *Council Bluffs, Ia.*
> *June 15, 1924*
>
> Dear Mother,
>
> This is your birthday, so Laura and I decided to write a letter. Have had a beautiful trip so far in spite of a few exciting times. We have met a pile of Calif. cars. Are getting a lot of advice and information. Our car pulls fine . . . have had no tire trouble or any other kind yet. The kids were dutifully cleaning the spark plugs today. A fellow who used to run a garage came around and gave

us what seemed to me good advice—that is not to fool with our car unless it doesn't work.

The tourist camp [here] is on a high hill—and we see Omaha right across the Missouri. Big place. Council Bluffs is big, too, about 250,000. Had quite a time locating the tourist camp. They charge 50 cents per car but it is worth it as we have free stoves all heated for cooking—water—had fine shower baths last nite that felt pretty good, etc.

It rained a lot here yest. p.m., but today it's sunny and a breeze is blowing, so I think we'll have nice weather now. This is Sunday morning, so we are loafing around. Think we'll go on this afternoon, as I imagine the roads will be quite dry. There's about 50 mi of pavement out of Omaha, we hear. Have been hearing some accounts of the [Salt Lake] desert so have about decided to not tackle it but [to] go north over Idaho and Oregon. S'pose will change our minds many times over but it's all rite to sort of feel your way. A bunch of campers here have a radio outfit, so we heard a Sunday morning service from Omaha right here in camp. Absolutely regular. You see all kinds of outfits in a tourist camp.

Marie

Dekorah, Johva
June 15, 1924
Kjaere mor,
Ve er nu in Council Bluffs. Yah!

Now I'll write in Englesh. Haw Har!

I took a bath this morning!

Bess is censoring our letters so's we won't write to anyone of the—well, you know—men. We've had a very nice trip so far according to my notion. I'm the garbage can of the bunch so get plenty to eat at all times.

We got to Council Bluffs quite late. Grace drove all day and was rather tired when we hit camp (real tourist!). It blew just awfully last night, raining too.

Gee, there are some sporty costumes in this park. Just now an old hen went past—hi heels and knickers! They shud wear boots. Yas! Well, I imagine Marie writes all the news, so I mite as well go jump in the lake.

Well, Ma, I s'pose you're hoping this is the last page. Today I leave the state. The first time in my life.

Goodbye, Laura!

From Council Bluffs they planned to drive two hundred miles but made only eighty that day. The concrete paving outside Omaha was a relief, but beyond that it just kept getting muddier. They put chains on and still got stuck. A picture shows a gray car on a gray road with a gray sky and two grooves in the mud, titled "Typical Nebraska scenery." Another picture shows a line-up of bug-eyed vehicles at the edge of a vast mud hole and is labeled "Nebraska mud."

After one particularly terrible stretch outside Schuyler, Nebraska, they called it quits for the day. "The Lincoln Highway was not too good," Zelma wrote. "We were tired of mud."

I imagine they set up camp in tense silence, shaking the clumps of mud off the side tents before putting them up, exchanging filthy damp clothes for merely dirty damp clothes. The bedding, wrapped in wet canvas all day, is damp too. Tempers are taut.

Grace remembered,

> By three days we were getting a little edgy. On this third day [Marie] says, "We better do something about this, we've got three months to go. We can't let this go on." So [she] gave us each a paper, and we were to write down the names of all eight, and write what it was that [each] one said or did that bothered us.
>
> I remember so well two things . . . Agnes always said, "Well, you can say and do what you want to, but I know I'm right." What they wrote about me, several of them, was that I was too shy.
>
> After that we got along real well.

When I started going to Iowa by myself, I spent most of my time with Grandpa, outside and laughing. Grandma Marie worked in her garden or cooked for us, organized family get-togethers, and found local playmates for me, becoming upset only when we missed dinner because we were pulling a calf from the sinkhole or when Grandpa brought in buckets of apples too rotten to save. She ran the show, but Grandpa was the show, and I was Grandpa's helper, his right-hand man, important.

I lost my first tooth the day I met my grandfather. Uncle Walter drove the old tractor into the yard when we arrived from California, and Grandpa was on top of the hay wagon. I could smell the sweet new hay as the white limestone dust settled and I squinted in the brilliant sun. Grandpa climbed nimbly down the clifflike stack of bales, his oversized overalls worn, torn, and stained. When he pulled off his hat to wipe his sweaty, chaff-speckled face, his hair was stone gray and his forehead baby white.

I ran to him. "I lost a tooth!" I cried, "my first one!" I jutted my lower jaw, pointed to the hole where it had been. He laughed and stuffed his faded handkerchief in a bib pocket. "I lost a tooth today too," he said, blue eyes sparkling. He pointed to the hole where his front tooth had been and laughed. I was stunned for a moment—unnerved. Grandpas weren't supposed to lose teeth. But his laugh was calm and amused, his hand warm on my head. "We have something in common, don't we?" he said.

Then he swung back up on the hay, and with a cloud of stinking smoke the tractor pulled him away toward the barn. They passed under a canopy of trees along the gravel drive, and I remember the kaleidoscope of dark and light rippling over the hay wagon. One moment Grandpa was squinting bright, the next he disappeared in shadow.

Grandpa was seventy-one years old and riding on the baler when the hitch-pin jolted loose on a steep downhill and the hay wagon fell forward. He did a quick push-up on the baler before the wagon crashed into him. I imagine he screamed and Uncle Walter stopped the tractor, but how do you unpin a man from a hay wagon? How long does it take, and what happened to Grandpa and his crushed legs when the wagon was pulled free? I know he lay on top of the hay to get home and into a car and finally to the hospital.

I don't remember hearing about his accident, just writing letters while he was in the hospital for a long time. I told Mom what to say, she wrote it down, and I drew the pictures. Sometimes I drew a deer for the word "dear" and an eye for the word "I." We tried to persuade Grandma Marie to sneak their greyhound into the hospital. Brownie surely had to miss Grandpa after so much time. When Grandpa finally came home, they were afraid Brownie might knock him over in her excitement. She didn't. She waited until he was helped to a seat, then gently put one paw between his legs and licked his face.

The following spring, when Grandpa was out of the hospital and feeling stronger, he and Grandma Marie flew out to California to visit us. His hair was suddenly pure white, and he walked with two canes. I lived on Alicia Way, and Grandpa wanted to know how to spell it, so we walked to the corner to read the street sign. One of his canes was black with an ornate silver handle, curved like a steer's horn. The other looked like a smooth chestnut candy cane—almost lickable.

I thought walking to the corner with Grandpa and his two canes was more fun than anything I'd ever done. We walked only one house-length in suburban California, but he managed to recite three silly stories. He collected them—jokes, stories, and songs scribbled on the backs of used envelopes. But he didn't need to write them down because he remembered them all and piped them up at the most opportune and unexpected moments. Like the four-leaf clovers he could always find. Like the red feather we found tucked in a decorative spoon after he went home.

After his accident Grandpa didn't farm or keep milk cows any more, though he still kept a few Holstein steers and maintained an electric fence. When I visited he wanted to spend his time with me. Someone else plowed and mowed his fields, but we tractored out to check the corn and chewed ripe wheat that turned gummy in our mouths. Once we found a meadowlark's eggs in a swale of tall grass.

We spent most of our time fighting thistles—cutting, chopping, and spraying them. My legs were never tanned because I had to wear long pants. When Grandpa walked, one foot pointed out and one pointed straight. When he was a little boy he followed his favorite uncle around the barnyard and walked toes-out like him until it stuck. "They fixed it when they fixed my leg," he said, and laughed. "This one has a steel plate in it now." I thought about copying him, but I didn't want to walk like a chicken.

One day Grandpa and I drove the old sky-blue Dodge Dart to town and traded it in. It was the model with a push-button automatic transmission, and Grandma Marie missed it for the rest of her life. We talked to the salesman in his shady garage, then crossed the street to the brand-new deep-blue Dart.

As we walked up to it, I saw there was bird poop all over the windshield. I tensed up. Bird poop on his new car—my dad would have been furious. I looked at Grandpa, but his face didn't redden, his voice didn't rise. He just looked up into the tree above the car and winked at me. "Sure glad cows don't fly," he said, and we got in and drove home.

Some days Grandpa's legs hurt and we just stayed home and listened to baseball on the radio. The announcers' voices were a reassuring drone of endless statistics, play-by-play, and personal-interest stories. Grandpa sat at the kitchen table holding his better ear up against the crackling speaker and puffing on a cheap cigar. It was the only time for that luxury. The cigar smoke seeped up through the heat vent into my upstairs bedroom for me to smell later as I drifted to sleep.

Fair time was the best time. It was only then that Grandpa and Grandma Marie needed two cars, for Grandma Marie went to town several times each day while running the hamburger stand. Every year Grandpa's ancient Chevy had to be tinkered into running. We hauled the toolbox out to the rusted heap under the plum tree. I handed him tools and ran the long cord to charge the battery. Later I sat pressed against him when we drove to the fair, because there were no seat belts and the passenger door flew open on corners. I loved eating cheeseburgers and pie at the fair stand and going through the animal barns with their sometimes overwhelming earthy smells. We watched the animal judging and chose our favorite cows. Sometimes the judges agreed with me, sometimes with Grandpa. He managed the Holstein barn, and all the old farmers ruffled my hair and said I looked like a good helper.

I never knew Grandpa was always in pain. He only said, "They were so worried about my legs, it took them three days to figure out that my arm was broken too. I kept telling them that it hurt." And then he laughed.

❧

7:10 a.m.
Mon. Morning

Dear Folks,

We're all ready to start. Camped at Schuyler [Nebraska] last nite. Rained some, but not much, and as we hear we have graveled roads we are going on. This part of the state is very flat, big trees and green grass, rich looking country. Don't know how far we will go, but will just move on.

Marie

The women passed through miles and miles of alfalfa fields. "I've seen fields so long we couldn't see the end of them," Laura wrote in a letter to Emma she began in Lexington, Nebraska, and finished the next day 150 miles farther on at Julesburg, Colorado. "It surely is a wonderful sensation to see a town away off on the horizon somewheres. I've seen real prairies now. Shucks!" To them it wasn't the cultivated Midwest or even the Great Plains, but the prairie. Laura and Marie grew up on the edge of the prairie. When ancient glaciers scoured the plains flat, they missed the jumbled hills and valleys of northeastern Iowa. The sisters could hike through the woods behind the bluffs, cut through the Wingers' south field, and stand on the point where the rocky, fisted lowlands were pulled straight. It was the horizon of dreams. Somewhere out there lived their brothers' and their parents' stories.

As a teenager their mother, Anne, left her home in Norway for a sod hut in the Dakota Territory. No one now living in our family ever met her. Only the pictures remain, old portraits in which she stands beside her husband but doesn't touch him. Her face is wide, with gray hair pulled back into a twisted bun and her skin weathered. Her lips are pressed into a crooked line, neither grim nor self-conscious but bluntly present behind the bastion of breasts, the pose just another chore to endure before moving on to the next.

Anne's three brothers were already homesteaders in America when her mother died, leaving Anne and her elderly father alone in Norway. In 1879 they left the mountains, cliffs, and blue-water fjords of a land dominated by the sea (even cattle were fed fish when times were lean) for a flat prairie described as barren, treeless, and windswept. In letters, her brothers were honest. There was opportunity and land for the taking, but it wasn't easy, or pretty.

Anne spent little time questioning her choice. She was too seasick on the boat. Marie noted, "My mother was eighteen at the time she came across in a sailboat. These people that were leaving Norway . . . were very poor; they didn't have anything, so they got the cheapest kind of place to stay, and that was down in the hold of the ship. So they were down there in the dark . . . and they were terribly seasick. She said she was just so seasick the whole trip that she would never [travel] across the ocean again. And she never did." America and this territory called Dakota would have to do.

As many Norwegian immigrants did, upon docking Anne took a job as a hired girl; she worked for a wealthy family in Wisconsin. She learned propriety and a bit of English and saved enough money for the second leg of their journey. Then Anne and her father continued west, moving from humid lushness into desolate openness, scenery at once incongruous and befitting a community of Norwegians, where English wasn't necessary.

Anne's brothers were among twenty-one bachelors living on the edge of the settlement. She and her father moved into one of their sod huts, a home dug into the earth and topped with living prairie. It was milder in all seasons than the wooden houses, which had only thin boards between outside and inside. From their door Anne could see no trees, no neighboring homes, only the golden expanse and crooked horizon.

Summer was hot, with temperatures over one hundred degrees shimmering the distance and tremendous black thunderheads that gathered for hours before sweeping through with lightning and pelting hail, shaking dirt loose from the ceiling. Winter came early, dominated by fierce wind and cold and the familiar chores of chopping ice, melting snow, and carrying wood. At minus one hundred degrees windchill, with wool chafing her frozen fingertips and nostrils as she worked, Anne began to feel at home. In winter you were supposed to be isolated, and work equaled motion, life.

But isolated did not mean alone. Though she could not see their homes, the widespread neighbors still came to look at the new single woman, sometimes on horseback or by wagon, often on foot. One visitor was John Hjelle, whose two sections of land bordered theirs. He later said about their courtship, "There was one family whose land adjoined mine who were about the finest people I ever met. Now, I was always told that in choosing a wife one must take into consideration what sort of family she comes from. Hence, when Anne Stumley came to America with her father, [I decided to marry]." Why did Anne choose him? His charm and ease with people, his college education, his two-section wealth, his proximity?

John noted, "At that time I had a little frame house 12 × 14 with a small lean-to 8 × 10." There he brought his young wife and her father. "[For years] it was one of the nicest [houses] in the neighborhood," John continued, "but it was built wrong and was very cold." During winter nights, the moisture from their bodies froze solid in the blankets that covered them. John noted, "Anne always said . . . that the people in Norway were as well off and as comfortable as those in America."

They began having children—starting with four boys in a row. Anne fed them whole-grain mush and watched them grow. Later even her girls towered over her, with most of the boys standing well over six feet tall. John wanted his sons, whom he referred to as "Ole and the rest," to have college educations, so they moved east to Decorah, Iowa, where John himself had attended Norwegian college. Amid jutting white limestone and lush, rolling green, Anne bore the rest of their eleven children, one of whom died, and they made their final home.

Marie once commented that Anne "had her head more in the game" than her father, who admitted that shortly after immigrating he spent the last of his money on cigars just to "find out what it [was] like to be entirely broke in a strange country." Still, the children all knew their father well and had long, laughter-filled conversations with him while Anne diapered and nursed babies, raised vegetables and poultry, did laundry without plumbing, cooked over a wood fire, and was the spinning hub that family life revolved and evolved around.

Despite living in America for almost fifty years, she never really learned English, though she understood more than she spoke. She could communicate well enough to say hello or buy flour, but not to chat. She didn't chat. Even her leisure was defined by work. Marie remembered that the "gloaming," or twilight, was Anne's favorite time of day, when it was too dark to work any more. But she didn't just sit. Even then, enjoying a quiet moment at the end of a long day, she knitted an endless stream of socks, hats, and mittens. She didn't have to see to knit.

I remember Grandma Marie telling how as a child she loved to hear her mother's stories of homesteading on the South Dakota prairie, while I was thinking that her own life on the Iowa farm held just as much adventure and difficulty. Grandma Marie and Laura's stories, much like the ones they themselves listened to, drew me out of my everyday life. Beyond this, I also believe that my little ember of curiosity and adventure was fanned in their laps.

Today my mother wonders why she ever made that long drive to Iowa so many times. I think it was instinctual: she felt most normal when surrounded by extended family, and I think those gatherings fanned her own famished spark. It was a sense of curiosity and adventure, a westering spirit, that drew the young women west in 1924 and that they reflected with their stories. It's an odd thought that traveling east would ease my mother's westering heart. It makes me realize that not the physical geography but the personal geography was the issue.

Although my mother lived across the West all her adult life and was the one who taught us to fling ourselves down the bluff, she was a Depression child who lost her mother young. My main impression was of her striving for security.

Still, I do remember that whenever a huge storm front was hitting the Sierras, my mom would drive us up to the mountains. Unlike most Californians, she was comfortable driving in snow, ice, and blizzards. Once the storm was over we'd be snowed in and have the crowd-free skiing of a lifetime.

She took us on weekend hikes, often carrying my little brother on her back. I remember tide-pool hopping with her among herds of howling elephant seals and playing hide-and-seek in bleached wild grass that was taller than any of us. Once we hiked to the top of a still snowy Lassen Peak and slid back down on our jackets. And summer after summer she drove us to Iowa. Sometimes my father would meet us there and help drive home, but generally he didn't. She did all these things on her own.

❧

June 16, 1924
Lexington, Neb.

Dear Emma:

　Well, old cackleberry, seeing as how you are aging rapidly, I shall proceed to pencil you a short epitaph! Yah!

We are roosting in a tourist camp, showers and everything. Just now the owner ankled along and asked which one of us kids wanted to be called at 3:00 [a.m.]—of course they all knew it was I—but it wasn't—no indeedy.

We had a little hard luck this morning; the other car, not ours, got stuck and had to be pulled out—we kids were about a mile ahead of them so weren't aware of it until later. Gee! We think the road up ahead is still worse and we might get stuck again.

People have been very nice to us so far. Folks ask us if we carry a gun and we glibly answer "yes." Just now two boys are helping us. Western folks are good sports all right. It seems so funny to talk to some Califawnia folks. One told us today that we had a "haad jant ahead." Regular pioneers for you. It's awfully interesting.

Today we saw a potato patch as big as Solums' field. So long till we get stuck again.

We aren't stuck again; far from it. We've been going over swell roads the last 30 or 40 miles. A few miles east of Platte we crossed the Platte River. It's awfully wide and has sand bars all over. The water is just full of sand, fairly yellow with it.

The two boys [from New York] that helped us clean our spark plugs way back are staying rite with us. They burned out their bearings so are

stalled at the camp here. You see I am *finishing*
this *here now* or you'll *never* get it! See!
   Goodbi

   Luff from Laura
   Birthday Greetings! Thank you.

It was Laura's birthday too. She was twenty years old.

In North Platte, Zelma noted in her journal that the sandy water was "too fierce to drink." The two boys from New York showed them how to lift their floorboards to tighten their brakes. The wooden floorboards rested under a floor mat on the driver's side, not attached to anything. One of the boys tied a long string to an open wrench and tightened the brake bands with it. The string, he explained, was in case you dropped the wrench. Otherwise it would be lost in the transmission below. Marie's photo, labeled "Spark plug experts," shows them grinning from a customized open truck, called a "bug," their hatless white foreheads contrasting with sun-darkened cheeks.

As the women continued west they gradually gained altitude, and the landscape seemed to expand as it faded from green to blond. Zelma wrote, "Western Nebraska scenery was fascinating. The wind had blown out the tops of some of the hills, and we saw remnants of old sod houses made by the pioneers." What a place to live, she thought. What a wind. Marie remembered her father's story of an ox stepping through his sod ceiling, and another time when it scratched its neck on the chimney and shook dirt into the frying food. Laura had a different perspective. "Just now the engine began to miss," she wrote to Emma, "so Magnesium and Grease Spot [Agnes and Grace] piled out to remedy the evil and cured it immediately. Spark plugs are simple! Yas!"

In 1924 the Lincoln Highway cut across Nebraska to Wyoming, following the California-Oregon wagon trail west. But because the route had moved over time, sometimes north and sometimes south, maps and signs were confusing. At Big Springs, where the road to Denver left the Lincoln Highway and cut south along the South Platte River valley, summer road construction added further uncertainty. Each of the cars followed its "Blue Book," which consisted of written instructions based on landmarks (like "Turn right at the yellow house with two elm trees") rather than a map. When people repainted their homes a new color, it confused drivers.

Martha was driving Ophelia. "She was not a very good driver," Marie said. "She didn't have much confidence in herself. . . . Martha had her turn driving; she was no good, you know, but she was supposed to have her turn." Outside Julesburg, Colorado, she lost the road completely and started across a field. Suddenly, with a loud bang, the car jolted to a stop. It was their first blowout.

"Tires didn't last long," Marie noted. Flat tires were the main mechanical problem of Model T travel, and Marie reported on their tires in nearly every letter home. In Ophelia the women carried a tool kit under the rear seat, complete with pump, jack, and patching materials. They had to jack the car up, remove four lug nuts, and pull the rim and tire from the spoked part of the wheel. This one was badly blown, so they substituted the spare rim and tire from the back of the car. Normally, a flat would simply be patched.

"We had to change tires every once in a while," Marie remembered, "and then we had such a cumbersome way of doing it." This was because Marie did not buy a jack. "[It] cost a little money," she noted, "so we were going to get along without that." It isn't clear just how they accomplished this. Some old-timers contend that any average man or strong woman could lift one side of a Model T while someone else wedged a brace under the side—often just a thick board. Others insist that a long lever was necessary. None of the women could remember how they raised the car without a jack, though Marie recalled that her brother Walter "built us some sort of contraption" and that changing tires with it "was difficult." Whether it was lifting a side herself or using a lever, everyone remembered that Laura changed the tires.

∽

Driving to church when I was fifteen or so, Grandma Marie pulled off the highway. It was just the two of us. Grandpa had gone early for a choir rehearsal. "Why are we stopping?" I asked.

"We have a flat tire."

I had heard nothing, felt nothing. "How do you know?"

"I've had them before," she said.

She was so nonchalant. She didn't even jump or look around or say "shit" or anything, just calmly pulled to the side. Now what? I couldn't remember ever having a flat tire before, but I could remember when the fan belt broke in our tan VW. Dad fixed it. It took forever. My sister and I had to stay in the hot car while traffic whizzed past on the California freeway, shivering the whole car. Dad was tense; he wasn't handy. He preferred to pay other people to fix things. Mom was tense too; he should have been handy. She didn't like always paying other people, and his being edgy now was his fault too. And how was she supposed to know where the god-damn manual was? My sister and I sat in the back seat and sweated and hoped they wouldn't scream at each other. We jumped every time the car shook. Eventually, surprisingly, after much banging of tools and knuckles, it was fixed and we went on. I don't remember anything else about that day.

Now here I was with my ancient grandmother and a flat tire. What would we do?

We both got out of the car; there was no traffic on the Iowa highway. The flattened tire looked like an ice cream bar melting on the hot pavement. She walked back and opened the trunk, got out the jack and the lug wrench and loosened the lug nuts. I watched in amazement. It seemed so easy.

Just then a loud old pick-up truck pulled up behind us, tires crunching and popping gravel. It was the toothless man who ran the dump. Grandma Marie deferred to him; she was wearing her church dress, after all, but she was impatient and he talked and giggled too much. Plus, whenever he spoke he spit on us. But he knew what he was doing too and eventually closed the trunk with a puff of powdery white dust. We got to church on time.

That night I asked if I could try changing a tire myself. Grandma Marie said, "Yes, but in the pasture." It was their new car, the deep-blue Dodge Dart. I took down the electric fence, found first gear, and drove to the flattest spot I could find. Then I found the trunk key and for the first time blinked at the white puff of limestone-scented dust when the lid opened. Years later Grandma Marie gave me that car after she stopped driving. I took it home to Montana, but the puff of limestone whenever I opened or closed the trunk never went away.

I attached the jack to the special slot in the bumper and jacked the car up, its frame creaking as the long metal handle became harder to hitch. I broke the lug nuts free and removed the wheel. Then I put it back on, snugging the bolts with the jack handle, learning what is tight enough but not too tight. I lowered the car and removed the jack. Then I did it again, and again.

Grandma Marie and Grandpa were in the house. I don't know if they watched me and laughed together or if they wondered what I thought I was doing. When my mom was four years old she found a screwdriver and removed all the lower kitchen cabinet doors, so my wanting to take things apart wasn't all that unusual.

At the time I just wanted to know how to change a tire so next time I could fix it myself. But there was a certain Zen in taking it off and putting it on, in pushing down the anxiety that I might do it wrong, that the jack might pop out and hit me and the car thunk to the ground. I savored the warmth of the lug nuts and wrench in my hands, the metal hard enough to hurt. Over and over I changed that tire. Now when I picture myself, a scrawny blonde in the waning light tugging the hard rubber into place, I realize that I was embracing the calm. I not only wanted to know how to change a tire, I wanted to be calm, like Grandma Marie.

❧

Martha made it to the next town on the spare. Then she got flustered and confused and struck another car. Marie couldn't understand it. Only two other vehicles on the road, and Martha managed to hit one of them. Luckily she wasn't going fast enough to do much damage, and no one was hurt. They continued with a bent fender.

"Not a tree or cloud but plenty of sun," Zelma wrote of the sun-struck, silent vastness and increasing elevation. All across the flat part of eastern Colorado the sun was relentless, and the lush humidity of Iowa and Nebraska changed to the dry, thin, sunburned air of the high prairie. Zelma noted any shade they found with underlines and exclamation marks. Bess's curls became almost manageable. "Pop, cowboys, cranes, yellow sky, no shade," Zelma wrote. In a letter home Laura noted, "Most of us have acquired a healthy coat of brown by this time, me included. Some have acquired sunburned noses and are a refreshing sight indeed (me not included)."

Sterling, Colo.
Tues. Evening

Dear Emma,

At last we are in Colorado, about 150 mi. from Denver. Will get there some time tomorrow. Roads are wonderful as soon as we struck this state. They certainly were fierce across a lot of Nebraska. S'pose Laura gave u the particulars as she was writing when we came thru this forenoon. Anyway our Ford pulled rite thru. We surely are having a lot of fun out of this and good luck too.

Out here there isn't much rain. Guess it won't rain tonite. Has stormed for the last three nights so we've had plenty of experience along that line. We saw a lot of irrigation ditches this afternoon. Alfalfa and sugar beets seem to be the main crops. This is pretty country so far—much more so than Neb.

Marie

For two more days they drive, clinging to the hot shade inside the cars, watching piles of white clouds hover on the western horizon, wondering when they will reach their cool promise.

From Iowa

Outside Goodrich I imagine the two cars bouncing in close tandem over a rocky section of road. Suddenly Zelma gasps and hits the brakes, forcing Marie to do the same. Before anyone can even exclaim, Zelma leaps out of her car into the middle of the dusty road, a hot wind flapping her shirtsleeves. She doesn't point, doesn't speak—just stands there, staring into the distance. This behavior, without commentary, is odd for Zelma. One by one the others join her, squinting in silence at the shimmering horizon—at the Rocky Mountains.

3. We on the Pigmy Road

All the way to Denver they watched the distant peaks. "Mountains were something we didn't have back [home]," Laura remembered. "We rode across the prairie, and . . . off in the distance we could see snowcapped mountains. What a thrill that was!"

When they reached Denver, Marie wrote home: "This is some burg! The traffic here [is] nothing slow. They say there are no traffic regulations, and people speed around something fierce. We succeeded in getting through without being bumped, but some fellows from New York that [we've gotten to know] were run into [within fifteen minutes]. Needless to say, we aren't planning on doing much sightseeing by driving around here." In an interview she remembered, "We liked to stay out of big cities because we hadn't driven an awful lot."

She noted that they camped at Overland Park outside Denver and "had to pay fifty cents to get in, and not very swell accommodations either. Lots of tents here, though. We saw a cute papoose." Her photo of an Indian family is labeled "Navaho Indians, Denver." The next day was spent washing: themselves, their laundry, and their cars.

Denver, Colo.
June 19, 1924

Dear Emma:

We are staying here today only. Are going to drive the flivver down to get a hub fixed, as one front wheel wiggles. It will cost about $2, but we'll feel better. We've had fine luck so far, no tire trouble of any kind as yet—not bad, eh? Haven't been stuck yet, and except for having our carburetors need cleaning we've had no engine trouble. The other kids haven't been so fortunate. They have been stuck a few times, had a blow out and got off the trail and drove around in the wilderness a couple hours [yesterday]. We don't try to keep together any longer. We just decide on a destination and get there as best we can. There are so many tourists willing to help who can do so much better then we.

We each take a day driving so we don't scrap. The others had quite a time, as they all thought they needed practice. Finally they decided to let Christine get all the practice, [especially] in the hard places, as she's the most levelheaded one in the bunch. When Grace and I were driving, Agnes would do most of the work from the back seat, but we've got her tamed down so she doesn't try to run everything anymore. Christine is fine—she certainly isn't a bit like we thought she would be.

We had our first glimpse of the mountains yesterday afternoon. We were quite thrilled. At first it was hard to tell whether they were clouds or mountains. They certainly are pretty, stretching in a long range as far as we can see both north and south.

'Twas quite cool last night, and the kids froze. Wonder what they will do [in the mountains] if they freeze now. Plan to leave tomorrow morning for Pikes Peak and Colorado Springs. Guess I'll close now.

Marie

It was afternoon before they packed up and drove to Buffalo Bill's grave, which was on top of nearby Lookout Mountain. Nicknamed the Lariat Trail, the road was so steep it had sixty-three turns in seven miles. They counted them. "Bess swallowed quarts of air coming down." Laura wrote in her journal, "Grace drove, did fine." They photographed Bear Creek Canyon, saw Longs Peak in the distance, and camped at Palmer Lake. They had never imagined such scenery.

They bought wood, built a large fire, and ate supper huddled around it, wrapped in coats and blankets. Summer nights in Iowa are as hot and sticky as the days. You barely want a sheet over you in bed, and that just to keep skin from touching skin. Here they wore flannel pajamas, bed socks, sweater, and bathrobe and stuffed newspapers under themselves to keep out the cold from below. Being swaddled under a weight of six blankets, breathing cool air, was like winter for them. The smell of wood smoke on the blankets only added to the illusion.

The next day they headed for Pikes Peak. On the way, they toured the Garden of the Gods, known for its massive rock formations. "Everything was red," Marie noted. "That beautiful red rock is part of the scenery." She photographed Laura

We on the Pigmy Road

climbing the base of one of the sheer cliffs, like a dark spider on the light stone, her black shoes in sharp focus.

They continued through the Narrows and over the Serpentine Trail to the Cave of the Winds. Laura wrote. "The cave was truly wonderful, and I was very glad to see it. The guy who showed us around surely knew his piece. Another party was right ahead of us, and our guy used the exact words of the one before us, as did another guide in our rear!" At Seven Falls she noted that they climbed "about 300 steps to get to the top of some cliffs. Going down made one almost 'dissy.' These were very pretty too."

When they reached the base of Pikes Peak, Bess took one look up and had to sit down. Zelma wrote, "The passengers in our car didn't want to drive to the top of Pikes Peak, so we hired a car and driver for $4, got giddy at the top—for lack of oxygen—and marveled at the switchbacks." The girls in Jenny Pep didn't want to spend the money. It was Agnes's day to drive, and they all trusted that she was a good driver, despite the steep, treacherous road.

I decided I would never drive. At age fifteen, I was in an evening pre-veterinary class when an emergency case came in. The gentle little brown dog had been hit by a car and was in shock and pain, with one eyeball dangling by the optic nerve. It was slightly better when the dog was sedated and the trusting, terrified remaining eye went dull, except for the limp, rag-doll quality and that vacant socket. What had this poor creature done to deserve this? Gently the vet tried to press the soft, bloody eyeball back into the rigid bone. It was no good. He had to remove it. I ran from the room, threw up in the juniper, and never went back. I walked all the way home, determined that I would never drive a car, never risk an innocent creature that way.

Of course my mother had different ideas. She wanted my learner's permit in place before I went to Iowa for the summer so I could spell her on the trip home. Over the summer my grandparents would teach me how to drive, as they'd taught her. She told me how her dad, my grandpa, just gave her the keys to the hog truck and turned her loose in the apple orchard where she couldn't hurt anything. Didn't she realize I was facing a different world?

Grandma Marie and Grandpa considered themselves competent drivers, having done it for so long, even though driving tests didn't exist when they got their licenses, Grandpa couldn't see after dark, and in over fifty years of driving Grandma Marie never learned to drive in reverse. She simply never parked anywhere she had to back out of. Once when her car died on a hill and began rolling backward, she just threw up her hands and waited for the impact.

She taught herself to drive. One day she walked into the yard, climbed into her brothers' Model T Ford, and drove it. Or so the story goes.

The metal crank was warm in her hands. She settled and resettled her fingers like a batter hoping for a fastball, then took a deep breath and threw the crank up, spinning it with all her might. The motor fired, louder than she expected, kicking the crank from her cupped hands and knocking her over. It exploded recklessly a few times, then rose into a roar that sent her rushing to cut the gas. Behind the wheel, she adjusted the levers to a sputtering, surging idle, then paused, wiping her hands on her knickers.

Marie was fit, strong, and sturdy, like most country girls

of the time. Her soft dark bob framed round cheeks, and her wool knickers and cotton work shirt were pressed. She was alone. Mother had taken noon dinner to the men in the west field (brothers Walter and Albert and Father), and Emma and Laura were picnicking in the woods. Marie wanted to do this alone.

She released the hand brake, then pushed the low-gear pedal to the floor. The car chugged, jerked, and died. She yanked the hand brake back, her jaw thrust forward, and started over.

Ignition on, battery on, spark off, hand brake on (the sequence in her mind for starting a car too often included her brothers chasing lurching vehicles across the yard), choke, crank, throttle, deep breath, crank, throttle, spark, magneto, hand brake, low-gear pedal.

At last she lurched from the lawn onto the dirt drive. Low gear in a Model T was designed just to get the car rolling, and high gear wasn't much faster, but to Marie it felt like flying. The play in the large black steering wheel and the chuckholes in the driveway made aiming straight for the narrow home-made bridge frightening. Back stiff, hands tight, face thrust forward, for the first time she felt the terrain of the road with her hands.

At the end of the long maple-lined lane, where her driveway met the road, she thought about turning around, and the motor died. "Damn flivver," she thought. Flushed and giddy in the sudden silence, her soft bangs shoved back in a damp clump, Marie slumped back in the seat, grinning. She caressed the smooth steering wheel, smelling the worn upholstery, the engine oil on her fingers, her own nervous sweat. Smack in front of her sat the plain, angular schoolhouse.

A quarter mile from home, the school's crossroads was the

crux of her world. "It was that country school that saved us [girls]," she said later. Marie spoke Norwegian at home but learned to speak, read, and write English at school. Miss Hoime, her teacher, walked five miles each way to work, following the railroad tracks along the creek behind the school, the only clear route in the Iowa winter. The year that Marie and her brother Herman, two years older, graduated from eighth grade, Miss Hoime urged Marie to attend high school in town.

Marie resisted. "I'm a country kid," she said. "They don't go to high school." Generally they didn't, especially girls, but in the end Marie did. Going to school in town involved leaving home during the harsh winter months. While boarding in town Marie drank coffee and bobbed her hair—much to her parents' surprise. Once the long dark braid was gone there was no turning back.

When Miss Hoime stepped down, Marie returned home and took over the one-room school. Some mornings the woodstove was already lit when she arrived because bums had stayed the night. She never saw them. From the tall windows that lined the walls, Marie could watch her home as she taught. Even in the bitter cold she could see her mother hanging laundry or Albert chasing the Ford across the yard again.

Behind the school, Marie could see the creek and the railroad trestle where the swimming hole was. One blistering summer day when she was four years old, she followed a group of her older brothers to the swimming hole. They all stripped and went swimming. They were just kids and thought nothing of it, but when they got home and her folks found out they'd been naked, Marie got a whipping. None of the boys did, only her. "It was a double standard, of course, one I've run up against all my life," Marie said later. But the story, which she told and retold throughout her life, became

We on the Pigmy Road

a touchstone for her and always ended with the cry, "It was plain unfair!"

She sat in the silent car at the crossroads, her past and future and life's unfairness all before her. She could see no glorious destination; her determination to start and control this new vehicle could bring her only to more overgrown hillsides and stifling humidity. But imagine the sense of riding in a car rather than a horse-drawn wagon, the speed and distance available—and this time she was behind the wheel. Underbrush leaned out onto the crossroads east and west. Both roads led to town, but a larger West beckoned to Marie.

Her sister Laura always said, "Marie just had a yen." But Marie herself described the decision differently: "Early in life I decided I was going to travel and see things, I wasn't going to sit around like all the girls I knew. They stayed home until they married, then went into a house, had kids, and worked. That was all. I wasn't going to do that."

I got my first driving lessons while fishing. When it was too hot to do anything else, Grandpa and I went fishing. Digging worms out behind the barn on another sweet, sweaty day, he turned the layers of manure and I picked out the fat wigglers. If it was too hot behind the barn, we hiked out to the woods, to the cool spot by the sinkhole. If it was really hot, we drove to town and invested a quarter—those lucky city kids could just pick night crawlers off their lawns.

Then we drove out to one of our many spots to fish for the day. We hiked through cornfields and private pastures. Those No Trespassing signs didn't include fishermen, and besides, Grandpa knew everyone. I saw a monster one day, under a railroad trestle. I was alone with my daydreams at the shady pool. Then I saw a gargoyle's head swimming toward me, the ugliest thing I'd ever seen in daylight. I jumped back, dropping my pole. With a "ka-bam" the creature disappeared under the surface, and I was left to decide whether it was safe to pick up my fishing pole. Later my grandfather laughed and said, "It was just a beaver."

Some days the fishing picked up in the evenings and we stayed too long, trying for bass but mostly catching suckers for the cats. We hurried back across somebody's pasture in the dimming evening light, then I drove the Dart home, because Grandpa couldn't see after dark. I drove slowly on the gravel, neck craned, sucking in the rich smell of earth, content with the evening star, the drone of the motor, and Grandpa.

At the end of the summer I helped Mom drive home halfway across the country. One morning she was asleep in the back when I came to a long, straight downhill. We were in the middle of Nevada with no other car in sight. I pushed the gas pedal of that huge Pontiac Bonneville to the floor and held it there, gaining unexpected momentum until the speedometer touched one hundred miles an hour. I held it there for a moment, just to say I did.

At the bottom of Pikes Peak again, Marie took over driving, since Agnes was all in. They felt rattled and exhilarated and decided they deserved an especially nice campground that night—something with showers. "A car came up to us, [with] several men in it." Grace remembered, "They got out and gave us their calling card. They were very happy to see tourists coming and said, 'Follow us.' Well, we followed them and followed them, but you know there was no campground in sight, and we began to figure this was foul play."

We on the Pigmy Road

Everyone was already shaky from Pikes Peak, and the farther they went, the more nervous they became. Marie remembered, "I was scared. I thought they were going to lead us someplace and then do things to us. I thought, I'm not going to stay with this any longer, this isn't safe," and she turned around and hoped they wouldn't follow. "We just shook them," she said. "I'll never forget [that] sensation, because that was dangerous. Young girls out there had to be careful." No one wrote home about the incident, or about Pikes Peak for that matter. Only Zelma's journal mentioned it: "Kids got led away."

The cars reunited the next day when they checked for mail at Estes Park. Before they left home, they had made a list of certain towns along the way and the dates they thought they'd be there so their families and friends could write to them at general delivery. "We hoped to get some mail from home, at least," Zelma wrote. There was no mail, but they were advised to check again later. They went on and camped at Rocky Mountain National Park.

"Food and gas were expensive," Zelma noted; "25 cents for a quart of milk, 45 cents a pound for butter, and 35 cents a gallon for gas. We didn't carry large supplies of food in the Fords because canned food was heavy and our cars were already loaded. Besides, it wasn't really necessary. Even when we were far from civilization for several days we didn't leave the beaten path very far. Generally we could get food supplies at the little trading posts and crossroads in the mountains. We rarely needed more than a two-day supply of food, even in the National Parks." For the most part they ate on the road what they ate at home, though fresh fruit and vegetables were cause for celebration.

"Washed clothes, hair, and loafed through entire day," Laura wrote in her journal; "entertained campers with true Indian dance. Hallo Ella, Ella, Ella. Aa Nie Aa Nie Aa Nie."

Rocky Mt. Natl. Park
June 23, 1924

Dear Folks,

All in our party are fine—thank goodness.

I'm up all alone this morning, as it's too early for the rest. The sun is just coming up over the mountain, and it's very cold on account of the wind coming down out of the snowy mts.

I had a strange experience this morning. I heard a dull thud and looking toward the windshield I saw a huge animal. Upon closer inspection I found it to be a mosquito. Others of the same caliber were reposing peacefully on my face. Now you know why I got up so awfully early. Yas.

We spent Sunday traveling and . . . passed thru Thompson Canyon, one of the most beautiful spots I have seen so far. Cliffs rise hundreds of feet above one's head, an occasional pine tree breaking the monotony of the somber walls. A river shoots over huge boulders, throwing spray high in the air. We on the pigmy road felt our total insignificance (this does not include *me*, however). On the way up to this park we encountered a long hill. Agnes drove, so Martha, Marie, and I got out to push. The other car load are kind of scared to have Christine drive, no reason whatever, so Marie, Grace, and Agnes take turns at *riding* in their car, not *driving*, and of course it helps an awful lot!

Gee but it's pretty right here. Mountains all

around us; to the east are the pine-carpeted hills, and on all other sides are snow-capped peaks. I always thot that the darker parts of mountains were shadows, but now I see they are bare rock surfaces, with the snow lying in drifts between the higher places. I'm enjoying this trip very much. There's a charm in cooking among the pine trees that grips me. It really is fun.

Lots of people who see us come over and talk about Iowa, as they once lived there. People we've never even noticed ask how we got along since we left Council Bluffs or Denver or some other place where we camped. Oh yes, we attract a lot of attention.

Gee! I can't think of anything more to write. Here's hoping I've expressed my idea of these parts in the most poetic manner possible.

Love Laura

I didn't say anything about the Garden of the Gods. The rocks are a brick red, as are all the roads around there. The two huge rocks at the gate towered hundreds of feet above our heads. Myriads of swallows twittered and skimmed about their homes in these rocks. You see, the rocks are fairly honeycombed with tiny holes. Traveling thru these gardens we saw some of the queerest rock formations, all red sandstone (I believe). Anyway, they were a brite brick red. The heat was intense, the landscape rocky, [and] these gardens seemed to me to hold a million Gila monsters, altho I saw none.

Goodbye, Laura.

We saw a snowstorm in the mountains this morning.

The following day they got up at first light and hiked to Bear Lake, where they had yet another view of towering Longs Peak. "On our hike," Marie wrote, "we hit our first snowdrift, so we snowballed each other." She took a group photo and labeled it "Snow drift, June 25." Both Zelma and Laura noted the "mutt miners" in their journals, with Laura adding that they were "fresh." Grace remembered, "We had hoped to get some pancakes or something for breakfast, but they wouldn't let us have any. [When] we asked if we could get breakfast, they said no—it was all they could do to keep their [own] supplies. We were tired too; we'd walked quite a ways. You see, the atmosphere was so different that it wore us out, and we had to walk down with no breakfast."

Back in camp they ate a hearty meal; Laura noted, "Limited rations—almost," then they packed up and left the park, found their mail was in, and started to have car trouble. "We thought that what our car could do on a city street with four passengers it could do on steep mountain slopes," wrote Zelma. Ophelia stalled on a hill, and "we had to tighten our clutch and brake bands. [Then] the cupboard door fell off and we lost our cups." Finally they were towed into town with their bearings burned out. Zelma noted, "[It] cost $8.20 to fix."

There they learned that a twenty-four-hour vehicle count, made by the constable and his officers, showed that as many as six thousand vehicles passed through in a day, most equipped for camping. They also learned to always back partway up steep hills, so gas and oil could get to the front of the engine and everything would stay lubricated. Otherwise they would get "swedged."

They camped at Fort Collins, near another deep-blue mountain lake. A picture of the lake is labeled "Remember the boys' cabin at the foot of this lake, greedy we thought," but no one could remember why. Laura wrote in her journal, "Grace and I went swimming," but Zelma's cryptic notes, scrawled in the car the next morning, say "Grace and Laura miss curve."

"When we reached Wyoming," Zelma wrote, "Laura let out what we called a 'Rebel Yell,' but she [claimed it was] a 'Wyoming Yell.'" With the memory of icy blue water on her skin still fresh, Laura squinted across the dusty landscape and just had to shout. Wyoming was flat, harsh, and exposed, and everything seemed sharp—rocks, plants, light. Even the gritty sand was covered with tough, pointy little weeds. Marie called it dusty prairie. Zelma wrote, "We were hot, tired, and irritable, and the mosquitoes were bothersome. We quarreled."

Marie took a photo of dark bushes on light sand that faded to white as the horizon touched the sky, her shadow in the foreground. She captioned it "Typical Wyoming scenery: sagebrush and some more sagebrush." Another photo, captioned "Bravely lunching in the land of sunshine, sand, and sagebrush," shows the whole group sitting in the sand near a smoky campfire. Despite brimmed hats, everyone squints, skin reflecting as white as the sky. Grace's caption of the same photo reads "Just too hungry to pose."

Still, Laura was fascinated with the desert. It wasn't humid, for one thing, and even though it was hot and gritty, there was something that drew her—different from the prairie and less tangible. I imagine her with her pad trying to draw the details of rocks and brush beside the car. The more detail she draws, the more she sees, and when she looks at her penciled sketch she sees more than rocks and weeds.

Marie thought Laura should go to college to study art. As a child Marie remembered laboring over her clumsy drawing of a horse, while with a few simple strokes Laura had a galloping steed. But Laura didn't think of herself as an artist. It was just something she'd always done.

◠

Grandma Marie came to California to help my mother after my sister was born, and she wrote of me, "It's sort of hard to concentrate with someone drawing pictures across the table and keeping up a steady flow of conversation telling about the pictures. 'This is a ducky in a pond—he's swimming isn't he?' So of course I have to agree." I was the oldest, and the only child for nearly three years before my sister was born screaming with colic. She cried for the first year of her life, and in an instant I went from being a cherished solo to being background music.

I have one hazy memory of peeking through the crack of my bedroom door down the hall at my grandmother and parents in the living room. But I remember nothing else until my sister was two, except a few ancient and precious, almost mystical memories from before her. I have to think differently to conjure them; like seeing in the dark I have to skew my mind, relax into peripheral vision.

I am two years old and coloring. I sit on the kitchen floor and watch my tall, slim mother move between the stove, sink, and fridge, her skirt flowing around her calves from a wide, tight belt. The dress and her lipstick are beet-colored, and in my earliest memories she is always wearing them. I don't know if she ever owned a beet-colored dress, but I do remember my dad being so funny and my mom laughing so hard that beets came out her nose. They landed on the buff carpet, leaving a purple stain and forever aligning my mother with the color in these hazy toddler memories.

I draw Mom and Dad, using every crayon. Usually when I am finished with a picture I jump to my feet and wave it at my mom. She tries to be complimentary, but I draw so much. Still, every image gives me a thrill, except this one. I sit and look at it. Mom and Dad are smiling and dancing and colorful. Mom's lipstick is dark and huge around her teeth. But something isn't right. I look at Mom and look at the picture. I peel the blue paper off the blue crayon, start on the yellow one. Never before has my picture not been right. I don't understand it.

I look up at Mom again. She seems so tall and fancy, with dark, wavy hair, wiping her hands on a dishtowel and gazing out the window while the flour-smudged apron and long fifties dress swish around her legs at my eye level.

Then, suddenly, I know. They have no bodies. In my drawing Mom's arms and legs are erupting out of her large, smiling head, like Humpty Dumpty. Dad has no ears because his arms are in the way. I am frozen in amazement, intent on the structure of my mother. I stretch out my own thin legs and look down at myself.

I take another paper from the stack and draw a roundish head with a long, wobbly body hanging from it. My whole world has changed.

∽

There was no paving in Wyoming, and the crushed rock roads, studded with hat-sized rocks broken and planed like arrowheads, ground their tires. Ophelia got a flat almost right away. "The landscape was as bad as Nebraska," Grace remembered, "if not worse."

Before reaching Laramie, Zelma wrote, "Had car trouble again. Our car stalled, and three men tourists from the Netherlands stopped to help." Grace remembered the men were flabbergasted by these women in the middle of the desert heading across the country, without a man along. They cranked Ophelia and got her going, then took it upon themselves to drive along behind.

By the time the day was over, both cars were well acquainted with the three Dutchmen. They were working their way across the country before returning to Holland. Laura wrote, "Three Dutchmen helped us drain our radiator. Engine boiled wonderfully!" Next to the entry she drew a Model T from the back, with a bare foot sticking out and an arm holding bloomers while three men in battered hats, baggy pants, and clogs watched. She captioned the drawing "John, Leen, Joe." Still, Grace insisted, "We never called them by name, we called them the three Dutchmen. We weren't that familiar."

The wind in western Wyoming was constant, and in Rock Springs Ophelia stopped to clear sand from the coils. Zelma wrote, "The Dutchmen wore handkerchiefs over their faces, and we wore goggles. They carried a gun, and we saw them shoot a rabbit, which they dressed and cooked for supper."

The following day Laura noted in her journal, "Awoke to tune of awful cussing on part of man camped near sink—at Dutchmen. The roads were fine for a way, but later an awful wind came up and blew sand all over us. Our faces were sore for a week after." At last they reached Green River, almost in sight of Utah.

> *6:00 a.m.*
> *Saturday Morning*
> *Tomahawk Hotel*
> *Green River, Wyo.*
>
> Dear Folks,
>   We stayed at an exclusive hotel last nite—some class to us. Oh yes. We have two suites each con-

We on the Pigmy Road

sisting of two rooms and a bath. Sure felt good to bathe in a real tub and sleep on a soft bed. We sleep like logs every nite wherever we are, for that matter.

Well, this is how it happened. We pulled in here about 3:30 and were enquiring for the tourist camp. A former Iowan who is running a hotel here came out and talked to us, as all Iowans do. He invited us to stay here—our hotel bill paid! See? Wasn't that funny? Well, we drove down to the tourist camp, had our supper and came back, and he was so tickled. We are moving on this morning. Hope to get to Salt Lake this evening.

We had some fierce stuff to come thru yesterday. Roads were quite smooth, but we faced a strong west wind all day. Dust and sand blew so we could hardly see the road. We had our sweaters buttoned up tite and our red [handkerchiefs] tied over our faces. Our suitcases had sand in 'em last nite, so you see the idea of a bath sounded good. We are leaving now.

Marie

Kids had another puncture yesterday. Three young Hollanders who feel sort of responsible for us had five. We had none.

Grace remembered that the hotel owner insisted that both carloads stay at his hotel. "He invited us all . . . he said, '[The cowboys here] love to have a lot of women in their crowd.'"

The next morning they rose early and left him a thank you note. After waffles for breakfast at the Red Feather Café, the women packed up in high spirits. On the back of Ophelia they found a note: "No need a Man (Except in Trouble)," written in the dust by the Dutchmen.

The wind had abated, but now the roads were rough. At Evanston, they bought Ophelia a new tire and tube for a whopping $12.75. Her inner tube simply couldn't hold another patch. When they discovered the three Dutchmen would soon be leaving their company, they decided to cook them a meal. Excited by their plan, they bought cherries and invited the men to supper. Surprised and pleased, the Dutchmen brought along three potatoes roasted in coals, and everyone shared.

Despite the singing and card games around the table, Laura found herself wandering off into the silent distance. A subtle whisper stirred in her as she breathed in the dusty smell of sage—perhaps a premonition of her future, galloping her horse through the purpling desert twilight. Later in her life when Laura took a job in Phoenix, she claimed it was to escape Iowa winters. But perhaps it was her memory of desert evenings that closed the deal.

Laura came back to camp after dark, led by laughter and shadows around the fire. The Dutchmen planned to leave early the next morning, and everyone was saying good-bye when Laura appeared. They never expected to see each other again.

Grandma Marie and Grandpa kept a pony on their farm for any of the cousins brave enough to ride her. She was large for a pony but too small to be a horse, and she must have been black at one time to earn the name Black Beauty. By the time I knew her, she had faded or sunburned into plain Beauty. She had big, warm brown eyes, delicate nostrils, and a dished face reminiscent of the Arabian steeds that ten-year-old girls worship. But she was too smart for her own good, and ornery.

I was the only cousin who rode her. I suspect I was the only one at least as stubborn as she was. It was work to catch her, to saddle her, and to make her go. I remember hiding behind Grandpa as he tightened the cinch. With each pull she lunged as if to bite him, but she never did, and he just laughed. "You crazy nut," he said, cuffing her affectionately. Once he went out and looped a rope around her neck, then jumped aboard for a bareback ride to the barn. But she had the trick of making a quick turn when running full tilt, and she sent Grandpa flying while she galloped the other way. He came home laughing, but limping, and after that I had to catch her myself.

I never hid the bridle from her, never tempted her with grain. These things didn't work. I simply followed her around and around the pasture until she realized I wasn't going to give up and decided avoiding me was more work than it was worth. She preferred it when I held the bit out for her to accept instead of shoving it in her mouth. Then she would lower her head so I could slip the leather headstall behind her ears. I rode bareback, wearing the stains of sweat and horse-hair on my jeans like a badge, and we headed off to meet Cindy, my summertime friend who lived up the road and also had a pony. That first year, when Cindy and I were ten, my grandmother claimed we were two peas in a pod, except my hair was blond and hers brown, my pony black and hers spotted. Uncle Herman showed us how to hug tight gates open and closed, and then we galloped everywhere.

While I got to spend summers on the farm with my grand-parents, Cindy lived with hers all the time. Her grandfather raised Holstein cattle, pigs, and hay and let the county mine gravel from his quarry. One morning one of his cows didn't come in at milking time, so we took his new four-wheel-drive jeep out to look for her. He drove it straight up a hill but didn't quite make it, and we coasted backward to the bottom. As we continued our search, we passed an old stock car that sat rusting in a valley. Cindy's cousin who owned it was in Vietnam. At last we found the cow in some underbrush, with her new twin calves. We wrapped them in burlap and held them in the back of the jeep as we led their mother home. They lay still, born too early but alive.

I learned Cindy's story in bits and pieces over time. My family's version: her mother was too young to raise her by herself. Cindy's version started with her baby pictures. They all showed only her head, because she wore a body cast. She was born with her hips out of their sockets; she endured surgery after surgery to try to fix them but still limped. She called her mother Mary Jane; her father died in a war before she was born. I filled in for myself how much her mother must have loved him. I assumed it was World War II, because that was the war of romantic love stories, but years later I realized that it was Korea and that Cindy's parents had never married.

Summers blurred together with us riding sidesaddle at a bareback gallop only to slip off and land running. Cindy and I watched news of Woodstock on TV: skinny-dipping hippies fleeing the lake and the camera, with no underwear under their quickly donned clothing. The pasture creek in the woods was as close as we got to copying them, the rough seams of jeans pockets and burning-hot metal snaps unfamiliar on our skins. Then came another summer and another surgery, and Cindy was in a cast from armpit to ankle. She rolled around the house on a special dolly her grandfather made. We played cards and spun records, and I envied her makeup table with all its little bottles. Later we rode in the hay wagon while her cousin Tom stacked hay and Cindy's dog followed, killing mice in the stubble. Tom was a little older than we were, tall and blond and handsome, with the earned assurance of a farm kid. I was afraid to speak to him.

At the end of every summer I wondered about the next. Would Cindy still be there? Would we still connect? Then she moved to Minnesota to live with Mary Jane. When I saw her next she still limped, but she wore shiny crushed cords and thick eye shadow and smoked broken cigarettes hidden in her makeup case. She called Mary Jane Mom, for no other word could hold the contempt. Still hiding behind glasses, braces, and long pigtails, I envied her boldness. I had grown four inches that summer, and all my pants were too short.

We went to the Friday night stock car races. When Tom won his race we joined the thronging fans on the dark field, watched older girls scream past on hot engine hoods, stood together among racing motors and swooping, blinding headlights.

⤳

"Had first puncture 100 mi. from Salt Lake," Laura wrote. "I turned on lights with my big toe." They left Wyoming and headed down a steep, narrow canyon, emerging as if into a wave of heat and light. In the distance they could see Salt Lake City, and beyond it the shimmering white heat of the Great Salt Lake desert. Zelma noted, "We saw seagulls before we reached Salt Lake City. A great wide street stretched up to the capitol. It was a relief to hit pavement."

They reached camp in the morning, unloaded their gear, and headed into the city for an organ concert—only to find they weren't given on Sunday. Instead, they listened to a

Mormon official explaining his religion. A gentleman nearby asked questions, and Marie wrote, "Soon the two were extremely huffy, but exceedingly polite about it." Laura noticed another man staring at their group. She nudged Agnes and said, "There's a Mormon looking for a nice juicy wife." All eight laughed, and the man fled.

Salt Lake City
Sunday, June 29

Dear Folks,

We camped at Ogden last evening and came here this morning. The street traffic isn't bad at all. Denver was a fright. They have a couple blocks with a high wall around it containing all their buildings etc. It is a beautiful outfit. They said we could come to the concert tomorrow and after that a guide would show us all over the place. We are quite interested in what we will see and hear tomorrow.

We went thru the state capitol this afternoon. It is all marble inside—much more elaborate than the one at Denver. A guide took us into the gov. reception room and explained how much gold and other valuable stuff was contained in the furnishings. We drove around a while and landed at the city park. We saw ponds with swans and other things that go to make up a park—also got in on a band concert. From there we came back to camp. The other kids aren't here yet. They were planning strong on attending the Mormon services at 2:00. We figured we would be disgracing ourselves by going there in knickers, and we didn't have time to change.

This is a beautiful city—wide streets, lots of trees and shrubbery. The country around here is irrigated, and things grow luxuriantly. Salt Lake is in a valley, the Wasatch Mts. forming a Horseshoe opening to the west. We came thru a canyon, but roads were so good we hardly noticed that we were coming thru mts. Traveling yesterday was not so bad. Not windy, but roads were so stony—hard on tires. Had our first puncture yest. Other kids have had four and one blowout. We try to treat the flivver right. Change oil and test our batteries every 500 mi. Also try to drive carefully.

We have lost track of our Hollanders now. They were pretty good to us, coming behind and changing tires for us and picking up the potatoes that would drop from our cupboard. They have been in the U.S. about 1½ years and were on their way to the coast now, going back to Holland. They talked quite broken—were very gentlemanly, however.

We plan to wash some clothes in the morning. This is a pay camp, so there are good accommodations. Tomorrow we get our mail. Quite anxious for that, of course.

Marie

This letter is not quite so poetic as Laura's, but the scenery in a tourist camp is not very inspiring, u no.

They stayed in Salt Lake City for two days, doing laundry and touring the city. Laura wrote, "There was one temple which no one could enter if not of the Mormon faith and leading an exemplary life." Zelma wrote, "Red and green street signals."

They visited the Tabernacle, where Zelma noted a guide had them stand in the back while he went up to the stage, two hundred feet away, and "performed the whispering and pin drop experiment," which they could hear as clear as day.

They took seats for the organ concert, and the rich music filled the building. Then someone bumped the back of Laura's seat—Grace's too. Then again. When Grace turned to chide the tourists behind them, she was greeted with three large Dutch grins. Her cry and the familiar gruff laughter turned everyone from the music. After two days in a strange city, it was like finding family.

They invited the Dutchmen, who didn't have jobs yet, to their camp for another supper. They played cards and sang into the night, with Leen standing on the table to sing cowboy songs with a Dutch accent. It was nearly dawn when Laura led the women in "Good Night, Ladies" and the Dutchmen took the hint. They wondered if they would ever see each other again.

4. Echoes on My Ribs

On the way out of Salt Lake City they went to Salt Air, a pavilion built on stilts over the lake. "[It's] the summer resort of this place," Marie wrote home. "We're going swimming there." It was already over a hundred degrees outside, and everyone was excited about taking a cool dip in the Great Salt Lake. But the water was tepid and scummy, and it stung their eyes. "You can't sink," Laura wrote, "but you can't swim either. . . . my nose became filled with salt water and my eyes with tears." Agnes took a picture of the other seven in the water, all smiling, arms around each other, but Marie noted, "Got a swig up my nose that nearly knocked me out."

After picture taking, they had Ophelia's tires repaired, then they had to decide which route to take west. The Lincoln Highway across the Great Salt Lake and Nevada deserts was fearsome. The first 300 miles to Ely, Nevada, was uninhabited salt desert, followed by nearly 350 miles of regular desert to Reno. With its combination of heat, poor roads, and isolation, this was the most dangerous stretch of the Lincoln Highway. Zelma wrote, "When we reached Salt Lake City, we were advised that the road [west] was under construction, making it impossible to get through the detour without broken springs, for one could not tell when wheels would drop down into deep chuckholes." She didn't mention the washouts, salt marshes, mudflats, choking alkali dust, or heat- and sunstroke. "We decided to take the Oregon Trail along the Columbia River Highway, then down into California. We lost very little time this way because the roads were excellent except for a few miles in Northern California. Later we heard that the southern route, through Needles, had very good roads and we might have seen more that way, but people who took the southern route crossed the desert at night, to avoid the intense heat." Tires were a concern in such heat, as were complexions.

So they headed north. The next day Laura wrote, "I ran car six feet or so in low. Desert all about us." And this was the cooler route. Outside Snowville, Idaho, Ophelia had a puncture in one tire and a blowout in the spare. They had to drive the last fifteen miles on the rim. The town and campground were all astir over a holdup and murder earlier that day. The talk made the girls nervous, and no one slept well, especially after a neighboring camper had two loud blowouts in the middle of the night. Laura hid her purse in her stocking. Marie wrote home, "Have heard several stories about holdups lately, but haven't had any excitement along that line yet." She added that outside Malta they "averaged about 15 mi. an hour as roads are quite rough."

In southern Idaho they found that poplar trees on the otherwise empty horizon indicated a town. Zelma's journal reads simply "Desert!" Laura wrote, "Everyone [is] getting ready for the fourth. Camped at Buhl and enjoyed their dandy swimming pool." Marie's photo shows a wide, flat dirt road with low hills on the horizon. Barely visible in the distance, a rabbit is circled, with the notation, "One of a few thousand jack rabbits along the Snake River."

The next day, July 4, they followed the Snake River along the Oregon Trail route. It was their fourth day since leaving Salt Lake City, and though the roads were better, the heat and desert scenery seemed endless.

I imagine Grace driving, squinting through shimmering mirages and thinking that if she closed her eyes she would simply melt into the engine noise and hot upholstery. The Idaho horizon all around her seems as big and empty as death.

Grace's name was Grace Leonora, after "baby Grace," an older sister who died in infancy. It was a common practice of the time, and something she lived with all her life. Before antibiotics, some people didn't even name a baby until it was three or older. Grace had four more siblings die when she was old enough to remember them. That was why she took a year off from high school to help one sister with her sudden large family, because family was important but fleeting.

Driving in 1924, Grace didn't know that she would meet her future husband by saving his life. When he was pulled from a lake unconscious she resuscitated him, and he never let her go.

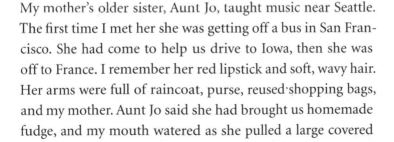

My mother's older sister, Aunt Jo, taught music near Seattle. The first time I met her she was getting off a bus in San Francisco. She had come to help us drive to Iowa, then she was off to France. I remember her red lipstick and soft, wavy hair. Her arms were full of raincoat, purse, reused·shopping bags, and my mother. Aunt Jo said she had brought us homemade fudge, and my mouth watered as she pulled a large covered metal cake pan from one of the bags. But when she opened it there was only a tiny bite for each of us. She had fed all the rest to her bus companions. "I gave them my blanket too," she said, and she didn't even care.

At our house, she went through the refrigerator and pulled out a big bag of slimy spinach; she spent the afternoon picking through it and saved enough to make a terrible cream soup that we had to eat. She washed my turtle's bowl with vinegar to make sure it was spotless and taught me how to find middle C on the piano. She wore green contact lenses (in the sixties) and made a big O with her mouth to apply her lipstick from a long, shiny tube, entrancing my little sister.

She described her home, a former chicken house with a big window that looked out over an emerald pasture with cream-colored horses to Mount Rainier in the distance. She climbed out this window to hang her laundry rather than going all the way around by the door. Once when a boy a little older than me misbehaved in her music class, she held him upside down with one hand until she was finished teaching.

When she washed her hair in our sink she got a splitting pressure headache—we didn't know she had a brain aneurysm. She died from it not long after. My mom cried when she died and again when she inherited several thousand dollars. "We were so hard on her," my mother sobbed. "Didn't think she could plan for the future. She was so different from us."

We started that trip to Iowa in the dark. The kids went to bed in the car in the garage, and Mom and Aunt Jo got up early to avoid the California valley heat. They took turns at driving our white Chevy station wagon with the red interior and at making bologna sandwiches and sleeping in the back with my little brother and sister and me, driving through the edges of the days, when it was cooler. There were no interstates then, just long lines of cars filled with heat and the stench from slow-moving diesel trucks moving across Nevada, Utah, Wyoming, and Nebraska. One dawn as Mom drove, my sister saw the sun rise first, so I kicked her under the blankets. But I missed and kicked Aunt Jo instead.

We stopped in the tremendous heat of Salt Lake City to eat lunch and tour the Tabernacle. Aunt Jo loved the singing. Afterward, she took us out for milkshakes (Mom was too hot to protest) but made us leave the last little bit in the tall, old-fashioned glasses. It was rude to make noise with your straw.

Later, driving east in the afternoon, it clouded over and the desert air cooled. Aunt Jo pointed out the window. "There'll be lightning there," she said, and there was. Aunt Jo pointed again, and another burst of jagged light appeared, as if from the tip of her long musician's finger. Time after time she nailed it, like magic, like Moses, like the home runs she hit over the pasture fence in Iowa, amazing all the cousins. No one else could hit that far, but she did it over and over and over again.

∽

"We spent the 4th traveling," Laura wrote in her journal, "and came to Boise in the p.m. The other Ford dolled up and went to a dance but we didn't— we feel best as tramps. We heard a man say that the only satisfactory thing about camping was that one could be as dirty as possible. We agreed with him! We celebrated by having an ice cream cone and watching the fireworks."

The next day, despite continuing three-day celebrations in nearly every town they passed through, they headed for Oregon. At the border there was a line of cars unloading gear for the border agents. Laura noted, "Halted for alfalfa weevil. We had to shake our bedding to get rid of any alfalfa weevils that may have come into it. There were a whole lot of tourists there, and of all the smart remarks they made! One dame from Mass. said she wouldn't have her bedding shaken where the rest shook theirs." Christine saw the line but drove right past and had to come back. She thought they were getting gasoline.

In Oregon Zelma wrote, "We drove through a dusty, windy sand-storm over a winding road." But Laura noted, "[It was] the most ethereal scenery. The air was full of fine sand through which the sun shone with a dull glow. One could not tell if the road were uphill or downhill if it were not for the hard pulling at times. We met a band of 1,000 sheep." Marie's interpretation: "We covered 266 mi. yesterday, the most we have made so far. The Oregon roads are smooth as a floor."

The next day they started down the Columbia River Highway, and Laura wrote in her journal, "The scenery wasn't anything to write home about." A photo shows two girls in knickers with nothing but giant sand dunes behind them.

Laura wrote in her journal, "We drove into the Dalles and had to turn a very sharp curve down a steep hill to get into camp. We got down all right and stopped at the bottom to register. As we stopped we saw the other car come at full speed, take the sharp curve with a jump. Christine grabbed the wheel and prevented their plunging over an embankment; rear of car skidded from side to side on loose gravel and seemed in danger of tipping. Zelma screamed and fainted."

Grace rushed toward the car, arms waving, but the car smashed into the registration booth. "What a disaster this could have been," Grace captioned a photo of the building. Marie remembered, "I said, 'That's the last time Martha's going to drive.'" No one argued.

Laura wrote in her journal, "We couldn't sleep this night."

The next day she noted, "Passed on to most beautiful scenery through great pine forests and along edge of Columbia River."

Columbia Highway, Ore.
July 7, 1924

Dear Folks,

We are ahead again today, so are waiting for the kids [handwriting change]—as usual. Marie started this but felt a tendency to close her eyes in peaceful slumber.

We are now on the Columbia River Highway, one of the most beautiful scenic drives we have passed over. I'm going to send a few pictures [postcards] home with this letter. (1) will give you an idea of the road we came up this morning; (2) is the place we are parked right now [Multnomah Falls]. Agnes and I went around these falls, thru a cave behind them and got almost soaked. It was just like walking thru a heavy rainstorm, and such a roar! (3) is one of the tunnels we passed thru on our way here.

Gee those kids are slower than molasses! We've been waiting here for about a million years. This is getting mountainous [*sic*].

[Handwriting change] We had to register our car when we entered Oregon. We have six stickers on our windshield now and feel pretty smart. We are beginning to realize we are a long ways from home. I realized it yesterday, and some of the kids said they did the day before.

The drive so far today has been very interesting.

The road is paved all the way. The Columbia is of a blue-green shade and there are mts. all along covered with pines of various kinds. There are a lot of big fruit orchards along the road—cherries, pears, apples, etc. As we have been nearing the coast the vegetation has become more dense. The trees are bigger, and there are a lot of ferns and underbrush. We found some berries that tasted a lot like raspberries but weren't, as the leaves were different.

We are about 30 mi. from Portland now. The kids were going to have the wheels of their flivver looked after. They mite have had to have something fixed, and they may be looking at scenery. This is a gay life.

They keep us a lot of the time—we console 'em with that our turn will probably come, but I hope not. We have had two flat tires and a blowout so far. Have bought one new tire, as one of our old ones was shot. Christine is the only reliable driver in the other bunch. Martha has been trying to drive some but can't be depended on, and Silence isn't very confident. Guess we'll have to relieve Christine occasionally.

Marie

P.S. The kids were okay. Had stopped to get something fixed on their flivver.

Zelma wrote, "Ten falls in 11 miles. Multnomah and Bridal Veil Falls were most impressive." The cars arrived separately in Portland, where they saw roses on every telephone pole. The kids in Ophelia found the post office, but not Jenny. "We thought we had lost the other car," Zelma wrote, "[but] when we discovered there was more than one [post office] in Portland we were soon reunited. We were at the wrong [one]!"

The drive from Portland to the California border was idyllic. Thick fir and pine forests shaded the smooth road, and the underbrush was as lush as in Iowa. Berry bushes loaded with dark fruit lined the highway. Bess's hair billowed back into uncontrollable curls. They passed a huge logging operation and paper mill, crossed a covered bridge, and drove on wooden pavement before reaching the "berry capital of the world." They downed handfuls of juicy blackberries and left behind all thought of the crushed rock and heat of Wyoming. A sign read Pickers Wanted, and they jokingly considered it.

In Salem they toured the Capitol, which Zelma labeled "dinky." Still, Laura noted, "the grounds were very beautiful." They waited in the shade for a ferry outside Harrisburg, eating loganberries and listening to a slow leak in one of Ophelia's tires. There were twenty-four vehicles ahead of them waiting to cross the river. They made 120 miles that day and camped in Cottage Grove.

As they packed up the next morning, Laura overheard two men talking:

"The Iowa girls are leaving."

"Oh?"

"But they are coming back."

"Oh!"

They had to go to three restaurants to find milk and bread for breakfast, and Zelma wrote, "We had to run for the car because we had gone to the toilet and [Christy], who was driving, became impatient." Laura noted, "Saw Laurel trees for the first time, also myrtles, prunes . . . " The sentence ends with a space left, as if to fill more in later. They left the Willamette Valley, and Zelma wrote, "Hit some mountains [and] had trouble with spark plugs. Drove four miles in low gear." At Grants Pass they paid twenty-five cents to have their spark plugs cleaned, and, despite warnings from other tourists about road construction, decided to head for Crescent City and the Redwood Highway. It was only a few miles of detour—how bad could it be? It was also much more direct, with Yosemite only three days away.

They camped at Ashland, with four other cars from Iowa. Zelma noted that gas was ten cents a gallon and the water was undrinkable. California, an Eden of stupendous fruits, was only a few miles away. Three days to Yosemite; it seemed unimaginable.

The next morning they prepared to tackle the 4,520-foot Siskiyou summit by filling and testing their batteries and cleaning spark plugs. Still, Jenny hit a nail, and Ophelia replaced spark plugs before reaching the California border. Laura wrote, "Up the Siskiyou Mountains, a beautiful drive over paved roads. Coming down we had a puncture. We're in Calif.!" Marie wrote, "Cool driving [in Oregon], but from now on we expect it will be getting hotter."

When the Model Ts crossed the California border, everything changed.

I didn't take art in high school. "Don't take art, take typing, then you can always get a job," my mother advised, apparently forgetting I'd already taught myself to type. (I thought writers had to type so their books would look that way.) It was just her way of being in the world. Even the smallest risk was terrifying. So I took typing and was excused from the

Echoes on My Ribs

first quarter. I learned later that my dad had argued for me to take art. He never told me, but twenty years afterward my mother did.

My mother was a fifties mom. She got a college education, then married and lived wherever her husband's career took her. She raised her family across the West in the only way she knew, connected to the welcoming arms of extended family in Iowa—a core that radiated across distances.

She went back to college once we kids were all in school. She took a computer class at the time computers were as big as my bedroom, their large reels fed by endless punch cards. She was filled with uncommon excitement and took us all to see the lab. Eventually she worked at Lockheed, where she was one of two programmers who had started out at a one-room school. She earned double anything Dad ever made as a research psychologist. Her job was programming nuclear submarines, which was a bit scary when you realized she could never find her purse.

Once I found a photo of her as a young girl, probably almost ten. Her long, dark French braids are pulled tightly back, and her pointy, thick glasses are large on her face, but she is still so cute. This is the girl who danced and giggled around the draft horse's hooves, even after her Uncle Walter told her to stop. "You just wait," he said. "Old Barney will reach right over and bite your head off, and then you'll laugh." Her reply, "With my head off?" It isn't the self-conscious adult photo face I've always seen, with head tipped just so, lips forming a word rather than committing to an expression. At age ten she has a lively spark of laughter in her eyes and on her lips. She seems about to move right out of range.

I showed the photo to my mother, and she visibly retracted. "Eew," she said. All she saw was the gawky farm girl she felt herself to be, the little Gertrude. Or perhaps she reacted to the image of something lost.

Two funerals in three months. Among the rows of resolute Lutheran backs and jaws, the flowers were the only exuberant things. Never more flowers than at a funeral—over the casket, around the casket, inside. People brought more and more, laying bouquets like abandoned babies. The scent, the heavy perfume of death, made young Gertrude's stomach roll, and this time it was her mother's funeral.

She remembered not so long before coming home to find the sitting room filled with flowers. She had never seen so many inside. Not realizing why they were there, she rushed in to smell them. The instant she noticed the casket, she felt her mother's hand. "This is a somber time," Emma said.

Her father, Willard, raised corn and Holsteins on the edge of Iowa's Washington Prairie; the ponderous black-and-white bull lived only a stone's throw from the porch. "Don't ever go near him," Emma warned her children. "Never for any reason go in the bull pen." But she ignored their screams when the rooster flew claws-first at their three-year-old legs, and when the goat pinned her son Billy to the barn, she brushed him off and sent him back to play.

According to her sisters, Emma was the pretty one, with her wavy hair and fine bones. They worried about her, isolated out there on the prairie, often alone—housework, yard work, farm work, and child care blurring together over seasons of changing labors—but Emma didn't seem to mind. When she married Willard, his father, Cornelius, gave them the farmhouse while he and his retarded eldest son, Elmer, moved into the vacant "house in the woods." Emma's home sat at the bottom of a long driveway, in the low land among the hills where water was easy to get. When it was built, the county taxed buildings for their closets. So though it had old-fashioned octagonal rooms, hand-hewn trim, and decorative lead glass, it had not one closet.

Fresh from her honeymoon, Emma was startled to find Cornelius at her noon dinner table, stiff and silent, fork in hand, waiting. Was he angry? She couldn't tell. He was so terse, so different from Emma's own gentle, laughing father.

To Gertrude he was just the old man napping on the porch. Every day he hiked over from the woods to do chores, eat, and nap. Emma packed meals for him to take to Elmer, who rarely left the woods. Elmer's methodical way of eating wore his spoon on one side, and because buttons were impossible he always wore pants with suspenders. They saw him occasionally, when they went huckleberry picking. He was an old man too, but a little old man. "Looks like rain," he always said. Gertrude tried to argue with him on clear sunny days, but he insisted.

Emma marveled how, at age eighty-five, Cornelius could still care for this son. But the old man nodding on the rocker, the grim lines around his mouth flaccid and moist, was a Jehovah's Witness and a socialist, a thistle in a vast field of Lutheran corn. As a younger man he had started a local co operative creamery so farmers could sell their product directly and—more unusual still—won a lawsuit over it.

It was a muggy afternoon when old Cornelius went into the bull pen. It was too hot to carry all that water across the barnyard; he'd lead the bull this time. Nearsighted Billy hung near the bull pen fence, not daring even to touch the outside rail. "No, don't," he whispered. The broad muscles of the bull's shoulder met Cornelius's hat brim as he grasped the brass ring in the wide snotty, tender nose. The smooth cream-colored horns pushed toward him, curving forward and down from the massive skull. It wasn't a snorting, stomping bull that struck Cornelius, shoved him, crushed him.

Billy screamed, and Gertrude turned in time to see the old man fall. Then Emma was there, breathless. She stopped outside the gate and grabbed a pitchfork. "Can you walk?" she called, her children clinging to her, peering around her long skirt. Then, "Can you crawl?" Blood dripped from the bull's snout as Cornelius dragged himself toward her voice. She said. "Gertrude, get your dad, in the south field."

Gertrude ran as she'd never run, those toothpick legs stronger and faster than she knew, the south field farther away. She saw her father's hat among the erupting corn tassels and ran through the rows, the wide, fuzzy leaves grabbing and cutting her, until she stood before him, bent and breathless, her heart screaming. "The bull, the bull . . . ," she began. "The bull pushed Cornelius." With that Willard was gone. Didn't say thank you, didn't say anything, just turned and ran for home. Gertrude fell into a corn row.

When Cornelius died, Willard hung the torn, stained overalls on a hook near the basement stairs. They couldn't find Elmer at first. He was studying the clouds, hands fast on his suspenders. "Looks like rain," he said. Then the flowers everywhere, filling the sweaty church and the house with perfume. "This is a somber time," Gertrude remembered.

Emma and Willard examined and reexamined the overalls, trying to figure out what had happened. They found a handful of corn in a pocket and decided that was the bull's goal. He wasn't vicious, just a cud-chewing brute. The bull wasn't destroyed, but the stained overalls hung in the stairwell for years. Gertrude always wondered why. Elmer was sent away to a special home, hands on suspenders, not waving. The house in the woods was sold and moved to a nearby town, leaving a thistle-filled foundation for future generations to ponder. Then Elmer was back, and there were more flowers.

Barely had they emptied the perfumed sitting room when a bed was moved in for Emma's father. In his nineties, Grampa told Gertrude, "I'm going into my second childhood." He was deaf, so everyone had to yell at him, though he simply grew quieter, paler, more befuddled.

Then, suddenly, it was Emma in the hospital. She had a breast removed, and everyone was hopeful until the pain struck her hip. She couldn't do yard work, housework, farm work, or child care anymore. The family moved to the edge of town; the children walked to school there, and Willard sold life insurance. Grampa moved to Laura's, then the hospital. Once when the children came home from school Emma made them a snack and seemed so pleased, but mostly she lay in her bed listening to their different life in the new house, feeling her pain spread.

Spring came, but Gertrude didn't run to smell the new buds. The scent nauseated her. Grampa was buried in the mud of snowmelt. Her mother would die next, and everyone would bring flowers. When the sky turned black to the south and people hurried into storm cellars to escape the wind, hail, and shifting funnel cloud, my mother hiked to the hillside overlooking the prairie. She stood in the tall, wind-burnished grass and let the thunder echo on her ribs.

Gertrude was fourteen years old and in high school. Her body was changing, growing suddenly, erupting like a gawky potato plant. She was no longer a child, but what was this hair, these breasts—sprouting even as her mother's were cut away. All the other freshman girls let the gym teacher know when they had their period, and they weren't expected to shower. Gertrude lied, coming up with an improbable cycle of whim and fear. And she prayed. But not for her mother to live, or for salvation or peace of mind. Gertrude prayed to begin menstruating before her mother died.

How could she turn to her father? Once when she soiled herself as a tot, he simply stuffed newspapers in her pants and waited for Emma to return. He knew what to do with a cow's prolapsed uterus—push it back in and hope the cow lived—but when his own children were born he waited outside.

Gertrude pulled the petals off a daisy and let them drop on the hard pew. She had watched her mother walk into the hospital on her own, and ten days later she had watched her die. Who would she turn to now?

I didn't go to Iowa the summer I turned seventeen. It was the first time. Instead, I got my driver's license, learned to body surf, and joined an elite girls' track club called the San Jose Cindergals. My life quickly became dominated by running and new friends. I missed my annual summer trips to Iowa, missed my grandparents, but I wasn't ten anymore, and I didn't want to lose any ground in the constant building of my training. I loved running, loved feeling strong and fast in my body. I loved racing with and against my teammates and seeing the constant improvement in my times. Then my beloved grandfather was diagnosed with cancer.

My mother wanted to take me with her for Grandpa's final vigil, but I refused to go. I didn't want to see him die. I think a part of me believed that if I didn't see it he'd still be there. Time and distance had always stretched between us.

My mother called when he died and gave the message to

Echoes on My Ribs

my little brother. He carefully wrote down that Grandpa was dead and put the note on the kitchen table as we did for common daily messages. Why she gave the message to him I'll never understand, but then my father just left the note there. He never sat us down to tell us, never took me aside to help me survive the blow. Looking back, I think he was afraid to; it blew his circuits to think about it. But he was the adult. Angry and hurting, after five days I threw the note away.

It was cross-country season when Grandpa died, and we ran long intervals over hills on rough trails in a September heat wave. My teammate Colleen's wisdom teeth were pulled that day. After every interval she spit blood. I threw myself into practice, hoping for complete exhaustion. My legs burned, my lungs burned, my eyes burned, but I found I couldn't run through this pain either, only with it.

In Iowa, Grandma Marie didn't cry at Grandpa's funeral. Her lips trembled, but there were no tears, her stoicism was that deeply etched. "I've never cried," she told my mother later.

"But that's not good for you," Mom replied.

"I know," Marie said.

After the funeral, I began writing weekly letters to my grandmother. As much as I missed Grandpa, she had to miss him more. She was my only living connection to the grace of Iowa, and with little other outlet, my grief and my feelings for Grandpa shifted over to her. I know she enjoyed getting my letters—she even answered them—but they served me too. Over time, and years of letters, I described myself and my life to her. Every week I took up my pen, and with Grandma Marie as my audience, Iowa as my reflection, I described who I wanted to be.

When they reached the California border, Zelma wrote, "Pavement ends." Marie noted in a letter home that while California had a two-cent road tax on gasoline, Oregon's was three cents. "No wonder they can keep their roads up," she wrote. They had lunch in a town named Weed, where Zelma's journal noted "saloons." Ophelia headed on while Jenny's tire was repaired. "We had a nail in our tire," Laura wrote, "so we patched a tube, brot it to a garage where the man said 'Good patch' and ripped it off like nothing. We're not discouraged at all—at all."

The road to Redding was under construction, and the heat was blazing. Without Wyoming's desolate distances, the sky, sun, and heat seemed closer. Grace drove slowly to keep the dust down and the carburetors, spark plugs, and coils clean, and because the road was steep and windy. Laura wrote, "Oh, the curves we sped around!" Marie wrote to Emma, "We came through a mountain range, a stretch of nothing but curves with no variation except up and down. 'Twas enough to make one see curves for a week afterwards. The three of us each take a day driving regardless of roads."

Zelma wrote, "Brick red dust was three feet deep for at least 40 miles, the last 15 mi. of which was detour." The detour was particularly unpredictable. The girls in Ophelia wore their goggles through billowing redness and choked and coughed along with their car. Christy took over driving for Bess. They ended the day with red raccoon masks, five o'clock shadow, and hair the color of Agnes's.

The girls in Jenny tied damp bandanas over their faces, but they dried almost immediately. In the middle of one long, exposed stretch of deep dust, they had another blowout. The heat and dust made them irritable, and Laura was tired of changing tires. She described the day as "a desperate ride." In a letter home she wrote, "M're says I shall tell you that we passed over 1,865,000 curves. Betcher life there are mountains in Calif."

It was 9:00 p.m. before they reached Redding, to find Zelma posted on the bridge waiting for them. Jenny was sepia-toned, and her roof sagged with fine powder. The girls inside were hot, tired, reddish shadows of themselves. "We rode and rode but never on the road," Laura said, but only Zelma laughed.

Zelma noted that it was a warm "Iowa night," and the cold showers were more than refreshing. After a good night's sleep she wrote, "Good looking station man sorry he couldn't put air in our tires. He washes our windshield, directs us through Chico." There they paid two cents for a meal of clingstone peaches.

Gradually the mountains succumbed to rolling hills and then to flat, sun-beaten valley farms. Irrigated land was green, the rest was bleached flaxen. "Here we saw real California scenery," Laura wrote, "We saw oranges, peach and pear groves, also huge vineyards [and] date palms." Marie noted, "When we were traveling south toward Sacramento, we took the right-hand paving instead of the left. This necessitated our crossing over the country about ten mi. to the right road when we discovered our error. We ran into the prettiest place where we stopped to ask directions. There were rows of palms and eucalyptus trees. The lady of the house was from Iowa."

In Sacramento the roads were paved, and though a can of peas cost fifty cents, four dozen fresh plums were only twenty-five cents. They toured the Capitol and marveled at the luxuriant flowers on the grounds, then took a detour on the way out of town. Zelma noted, "Hit rough pavement, wheels wobble." They camped at Stockton, where they discovered that Ophelia needed three quarts of oil. Zelma wrote, "125 miles from Yosemite."

1. The whole gang near La Mortle, Iowa.

2. Agnes, Laura, Marie, and Grace (*left to right*), with Jenny Pep and side tent. The number of windshield stickers indicates that this photo was taken near the end of the trip.

3. Bess, Christy, Mac (Martha), and Boob (Zelma) (*left to right*), with Ophelia Bumps and side tent.

4. Troublesome spark plugs and Nebraska mud.

5. Spark plug experts in an open truck called a "bug," (Nebraska).

6. Bear Creek Canyon (Denver, Colorado).

7. On the road from Lookout Mountain (Golden, Colorado).

8. Garden of the Gods (Colorado Springs, Colorado).

9. Early-morning hike up to Bear Lake (Rocky Mountain National Park, Colorado).

10. Bravely lunching in the land of sunshine, sand, and sagebrush; Marie *left*, Laura *center* (Wyoming).

11. Bathing beauties. *Left to right*: Marie, Laura, Grace, Bess, Christy, Zelma, and Martha (Great Salt Lake, Utah).

12. Sand dunes along the Columbia River Highway (Oregon).

13. Mountain roads! Pushing the car up what is probably Siskiyou Pass (Oregon.)

14. A herd of sheep.

15. Half Dome (Yosemite National Park, Californi

16. Camping grounds (Yo National Park, California

17. The Pacific Ocean (San Francisco, California).

18. Crater Lake National Park (Oregon).

19. Camp in Mount Rainier National Park (Washington).

20. Nisqually Glacier (Mount Rainier National Park, Washington).

5. From the Cliffs

"In early morning Zelma suggested that we make the Yo-semite before noon, but Christie said not. We all agreed that Christie has a head on like a tack, sharp end up," Laura wrote in her journal.

The road from Stockton was the worst yet. Zelma wrote, "Hair-raising road, 18% grade." Marie wrote, "Quite mountainous country." Ophelia had her carburetors adjusted, brakes and clutch tightened, and added another quart of oil. Jenny's brakes began to fail.

Laura wrote in her journal, "We drove over narrow roads on either side of which were steep slopes. At times we were within three inches of the edge, and those edges seemed ready to skid off any minute. At one time we even had one hind wheel over."

It was a narrow road, with barely room for two cars—and going up they had the outside, cliff-edge path. Marie remembered, "Agnes was driving, and [Grace] and I were in the back seat. Agnes was a good driver, but we had just that much space [inches] between us and that deep ravine, seven miles down. Laura was on [that side], and every once in a while she would show us [with her hands] how close Agnes was driving to the edge. We were just sick," Marie chuckled. "Laura [wasn't] afraid of anything."

Agnes took a break at the top of Priest's Hill, where they were told the roads beyond were even worse. At the next stop Laura wrote, "We had our exhaust pipe fixed, and a lady raved to us about how awful the roads were farther on." Agnes couldn't imagine that and suggested they stop.

Marie and Grace tried to phone ahead to the girls in Ophelia and get them to come back. The operator advised them to continue to Carl's Inn, the last stop before Yosemite. The operator then buzzed the innkeeper, who recognized the "Iowa Girls" in Ophelia at once and told them to wait. Though everyone was anxious to reach Yosemite, no one complained. They had just driven the worst one hundred miles any of them could imagine. Zelma noted the store had "angle worms, no butter."

Once Jenny arrived, they decided her brakes must be fixed. They camped at a National Forest Reserve near the road, which Marie described as "quite a nice place. There's a mountain stream close by and lots of big trees."

They went to bed early, but I imagine no one slept well. The night is very cold, and it's as if the bad roads had crawled into their skins. They dream of narrow, cliff-edged passages, switchbacks, and falling. Laura starts awake, only to have the same dream again. By morning she is rattled and exhausted. Agnes is sick.

I picture the two of them sitting together, wrapped in blankets, sipping hot, smoky coffee, while the girls in Ophelia pack up and head for the park. Behind the wheel again, Christy looks paler than usual. Marie folds the marcelled bed and hooks it back into seats, and she and Grace drive to the garage to have Jenny's brakes checked.

Laura looks around the empty camp, and the pit of her stomach feels hard. She feels worn thin, lonely, and sad—ill without any real physical complaint. She's never felt this way before. If only Emma were there. Agnes told her she was just homesick. Then a little black-and-white cat appeared from the brush. They named it Motorboat for its exuberant purr.

July 14, 1924

Dear Emma:

Well, as time is hanging heavy on our hands, I'll start that letter I promised, so you can see our present situation. It is peculiar to say the least.

We have had quite a few thrills since entering this state. The vegetation has been especially interesting. Quite thrilling to see the first palm tree—also the orange. There were vineyards composed of acres and acres all along the way—also rice fields and a number of things we haven't been able to identify.

We meet a lot of people who have been former residents of Iowa. Most of them think the world of this state, but so far we have failed to appreciate their sentiments. A garage fellow told us a saying about the Iowa farmers of southern Cal., namely that they come out here with a $5.00 bill and a shirt and never change either one.

Well, we came to within 20 miles of [Yosemite] and then decided we'd better have our brake and low bands repaired. First time necessary. The mountains around here were considerably worse than we had expected. The mts. we climbed in Colo. and the ones we had in Oregon weren't anything [in comparison]. Funny how [we've] heard the most hair-raising stories about Yellowstone and never a word about this.

The other bunch had started out, so after the garage advised new bands and informed us they couldn't begin work on it until in the afternoon, we knew we would be parking there that day. We sent a message with some tourists, informing the kids of the situation and told them they could either go on or come back. They hadn't gone far and soon came back, because it was pretty hard pulling for their Lizzie.

Marie

Zelma wrote in her journal, "Try for Yosemite while kids have brakes fixed. Got six mi. having pushed three times." When they stopped to clean a clogged spark plug, a passing car brought Marie's note, and they decided to head back.

In a letter home Marie wrote, "Several people informed us that the Yosemite wasn't much to see this year as the falls were all dried up. So [the others] were all out of the notion all of a sudden. Our mail was there, however, and everyone was anxious to get his as we hadn't had any for two weeks. Grace and I were the only ones that wanted to go, so we hung around the filling station and got a ride with a San Francisco couple. They had a swell Hudson, and we came sailing over the hill. I know our flivver could have pulled thru altho it would have been hard on it."

The car that took them was loaded. "We sat in the back seat on top of some mattresses and what have you," Grace remembered, "way up over to the window on top of [it] all."

From the Cliffs

But it was Sunday, and the post office was closed until 9:00 the next morning, so they stayed at Camp Curry.

The next day Marie wrote home, "All the stages out our road left at 7:00 [a.m.], so we are out of luck as far as getting back to the kids today. We have tried to get a ride, but . . . we feel rather nervy asking anyone to haul us over a *hill* like that. So we seem to be destined to park here till 7:00 tomorrow morning. In the meantime we can be seeing the sights while the kids back in camp are patiently (?) waiting for their mail. We sent a message to the kids with some tourists, so they wouldn't worry about us."

Grace remembered, "The reason we wanted to go [to Yosemite] was we had a mailing station there, so we wanted to pick up our mail. When we got there, they said, 'Well, somebody asked for your mail yesterday.' We couldn't think who it could have been, except . . . [a] traveler we [had] picked up and mentioned we were headed for Yosemite. It made us think, was he following us? And what was going to happen if he did find us?" Grace recalled being really frightened.

I turned twenty-one while backpacking in northern Idaho, in the wildest mountains I'd ever seen, at the peak of brilliant, thin-aired summer in the Rockies. Afterward I didn't want to go home, but somehow I could take the bus to visit Grandma Marie. Although halfway across the country, I felt close enough to Iowa to surprise her.

On the way I stopped in Bozeman, Montana. A track coach there was offering me a scholarship. I thought I wanted to stay with the Cindergals, but when I stepped from the bus into the dazzling sunlight and a valley rimmed with mountains under a wide sapphire sky, I changed my mind.

Then I headed to Grandma Marie's. The bus arrived in Iowa at night, and I walked up the hill to her house. She was in bed early for once, and though I knew where the key was I didn't want to risk frightening her by letting myself in. So I threw my sleeping bag under the elm tree and slept there.

She got up well before I did and finished her eggs and toast looking out the window at my pile of blue nylon. She wondered if it was a balloon from a nearby summer fair. I can picture her sitting at the kitchen table in the corner by the radio, sipping her coffee and caressing the tablecloth, trying to figure this one out. Then she saw my shoes and made out the form of a person in a sleeping bag. Some hippie was sleeping in her yard!

About the time she began to wonder if this hippie might be hungry, I woke up. "Why did you do this to me!" she demanded at the door before we hugged. We laughed about it later, but for years, whenever I telephoned the first thing she said was, "Where are you?"

༄

Yosemite Valley
7:00 a.m.
July 15

Dear Emma,

We stayed here last nite and are waiting for our bus now. We had a cunning little tent house all to ourselves, $1.50 each.

Both camps we have been in have had good entertainment. The one at Camp Curry Sunday evening was highly classical. After the program they had a so-called fire fall. Some one was on top of a high point and dropped a stream of fire over the edge. Sort of impressive, you know, to see it falling several thousand feet.

The entertainment at this camp last evening was more varied. Some jazz, some class, and what we appreciated most was a lecture on slides explaining the glacial formation of this valley. It is queer. Huge perpendicular cliffs on all sides. I like Half Dome best. The waterfalls don't amount to much this year as it has been too dry. We can see the discolored place where the Yosemite Falls are to be seen when there's water. Now there's only a slender thread coming over that you can hardly make out.

There was a lot of mail [yesterday], but none from home. If you wrote and it's been here as long as 10 days it probably was returned. We take it for granted that no news is good news. You see, we are behind on our schedule on account of going clear around by the northern way. We will soon be caught up, though.

Must close.

Marie

"Colder'n Heck," Laura wrote in her journal. "Agnes [and I slept outdoors], and M.B. [Motorboat] slept with us. Grace and Marie failed to make an appearance but sent a note saying they missed the bus this morning. People surely hear about us kids between the notes we send each other. Oh yes." She drew a picture of a small black cat with white feet and chest climbing a tree and labeled it "⅛ natural size."

They did laundry, cut and washed each other's hair, and petted Motorboat. "We spent most of the day—after we got a note from the kids at 8:30—eating fruit and playing the Uke [ukulele]," Zelma noted. Laura wrote, "We had new brake, low, and reverse linings put in, $11.00."

After a day of rest and a dreamless night under the stars, Laura revived and the sick feeling left the pit of her stomach. She wondered if she'd missed something important.

❧

"You always do the leaving," my mother said as I packed for college in Montana, "You don't know what it's like to be left." What did she want? For me to live at home the rest of my life? Here was this exciting adventure before me, and I wanted my mom to be happy and excited too. I went through my things, packed everything I wanted to keep, and threw the rest away. "It's like you're never coming back," Mom complained.

I moved to Bozeman in mid-September, the hottest time of year in California, and was greeted with sleet. On the first day of school it snowed, big wet, barely frozen flakes. It was colder than December in California, and I didn't have a coat or hat that kept me warm. I didn't buy warmer clothes and get on with it because it just didn't make sense to me. Somehow it wasn't real. It couldn't be this cold. I remembered the mid-summer dazzle that drew me there and kept expecting it.

I went for a hike on a sunny fall day. Climbed to the top of Sacajawea Peak in a T-shirt. Halfway back I borrowed a down vest from my roommate, and by the time we reached the car my arms were numb with cold. A few days later I headed out for a sunny run, this time donning sweatpants because I'd learned it might be colder than it looked. I took three steps before heading back inside. It was below zero.

I did battle with the weather. When Montana-born teammates ran endless laps inside because of cold, wind, and snow, I wrapped a scarf around my face and headed outside. I fell on wet-looking black ice and on streets without sticky snow edges, sported bruises on my knees, hips, and hands. One regular stretch was long, straight, slightly downhill, and completely open to high west winds. I was in good enough shape that when I got cold I simply ran faster, as my left side numbed and my thigh sprouted black shards of frostbite.

A new teammate brought me home for Thanksgiving. She was from Judith Gap, a small rural community where she graduated from high school with eight other students. Her older sister told of driving so many country kids to school in the old pickup that unless her little brother sat on her left she couldn't reach the gas pedal. During the summer, Cindy ran topless across the fields for miles and miles. There was no one there to see her.

When we arrived, deep snow already covered their ranch, which was surrounded by the Big and Little Belt mountains. I borrowed insulated coveralls and good mittens and rode on the hay wagon with her brother as he fed the cows. The unmanned truck hauling us was in granny low, its tires chained up even with four-wheel-drive. The cows came lowing over, their alfalfa burps sweet and steamy in the hay, the smell of manure welcoming. The next day I took out some cross-country skis I'd rented and headed across glittering drifts until I was out of sight.

❧

"Draped ourselves around until Marie and Grace came (without mail from home)," Laura noted in her journal.

Marie wrote:

> As soon as Grace and I got back from the valley the kids were ready to start, so we did. It was

Grace's turn to drive our car. Christine had burned her fingers, and Silence was afraid to tackle the mountain roads, so they wanted one of us to run theirs. Agnes refused, so I had to. Well, we came thru fine over the mountain roads that had been so scary going in. Some places it was about 3,000 feet straight sailing. When we got over the kids told me of an accident the garage man had told 'em. They were scared to tell me before. We went up that road last Saturday. A man had gone over Sunday and fallen about 200 ft. Was killed of course.

Jenny, with Martha along, got only a few miles before Laura noted, "Our brake bands weren't any too good, so we tightened them; then went back [because] we had left our dishes." Grace was driving. As she came down one short, steep hill, another car was coming up. "Of course he had the right of way," she remembered, "[but] nothing held in the brake. We turned up, naturally, off the highway, and struck a tree."

They waited at the side of the road while the other driver went for help. "We had to camp right on the ground in the open, no tents or anything, until the fellow [came]," Grace remembered. "He felt so sorry for us. But we weren't hurt, we could still go on; it was just the brakes."

Laura wrote, "A road boss pulled us out. We went [back] and had *new* bands put in ($7.50). In the evening the road boss called for us. He took us on to Groveland in hopes we'd find the kids, but we didn't find them so we went back to [camp] and went to bed with our clothes on, and to sleep." The next day they wrote to the road boss "and gave it to his partner. Har!" Grace noted that she corresponded with him for several months. "We really trusted him," she said. "He was kind to us."

Ophelia had gone as far as Oakdale (seventy-five miles) and spent the night at a free park. "No showers," noted Zelma. "Jenny had the dishes, so we borrowed cups. We made hamburgers and tomatoes and ate out of covers [buns]." Marie wrote, "[The kids] didn't show up at all, so next morning we got up, packed, and sat on the highway waiting for them. Hailed a tourist, and he said he'd seem 'em in a garage having their burned brakes fixed. We waited all day."

Meanwhile, Laura's journal reads: "Up at 5:15, off at 5:30! Our low bands functioned like mud! Reverse bands—ditto. Brakes good. New gear and brake bands at Groveland, [after which] our bearings burned out. It sounded awfully loud, and Agnes and I took turns riding on the running board to see if it came from the wheels or engine." They stopped again to have it fixed, and a passing car told them the rest of their party was in the free camp in Oakdale.

> *July 16, 1924*
> *Groveland, Calif.*
>
> Dear Folks,
>
> Just a few lines to tell you that *I* am fine. Marie went in the other car so I don't know how *she* is, but imagine her to be the same. We are having new bands put in our car for the third time and as a result are frothing at the mouth. Shucks!
>
> *Laura Hjelle*

They were told the car would soon be ready, so Laura and Agnes caught a ride to Oakdale. To everyone's surprise, they just walked into camp. But time went by, and still Jenny didn't appear. "We made camp and ate out of paper cups and plates." Zelma noted. At last Marie called the garage to learn that besides brakes and bearings, they had found a piston gone, and Grace and Martha had to stay the night. "After a lot of trouble," Laura wrote, "we finally got places for six of us to sleep in three beds." Zelma noted, "Four on two cots." At least it was warm.

> *Oakdale, Cal.*
> *July 17, 1924*
> Dear Folks,
>
>   Now begins our tale of woe. A small matter of three new sets of bands and bearings and what not.
>
>   Those cheats up in the mts. had put in bum bands twice—that burned out in a few hours, not in the least due to the driver's work either. I imagine they sting all tourists that way. They are alone up there—have no competition and don't care as the tourist doesn't come back, of course. Haven't heard the bill, but s'pose it won't be any small matter. We pay 35 cents/gal for gas up there and 40 cents for oil.
>
>   Feels sort of good to be on the level again.
>
>   [Handwriting change] Marie is sleeping off the effects of this letter. Say, you should have heard our bearings when they burned out. I'm going to wash my feet now, so I'll close. Goodbye,
>
>   *Laura*

"On to Oakland!" begins Laura's journal entry for the day. She made no mention at all of Jenny's return, or of crossing the hot Central Valley. Zelma noted, "Chris runs over barb wire, seedless grapes, coil filed and timer wire attached, 50 cents." They bought fresh fruit from little stands along the way and exclaimed over the variety of choices, and the prices. In the blazing heat, they had no appetite for anything else.

On reaching Oakland, Zelma noted that they drove past the lake and market and camped at the "East Bay Auto Camp, #259, on First Street," where a shed was included in the fifty-cent fee. She wrote, "We prepared for a cold night. Wore sweaters and bathrobes." They got up early, and while Martha and Zelma wore knickers, Christy and Bess put on dresses for San Francisco. "[Took Southern Pacific] Rail for Oakland Pier," Zelma wrote, "Sacramento Ferry across Bay. Buy tickets, $2.50, for sight seeing of town and China town." In her journal Zelma drew a space of water between two peninsulas, labeled "Golden Gate" with a question mark. "Most people expect to see a gate across here," she wrote. "So called because of golden light on it at sunrise." In 1924 neither the Bay Bridge nor the Golden Gate Bridge had yet been built.

The girls in Jenny skipped the bus tour because it was cheaper to drive to the pier and ferry their car across the bay with them. It was Agnes's day to drive.

"We're crossing the San Fran Bay!" Laura wrote, "Frisco next!" Of their day she wrote, "We see the Pacific, also an army private *guarding* two K.P.'s but *watching* us—Marie and Grace take his picture. Marie, Grace, and Agnes waded in the Pacific. Huge waves dash upon the rocks along the coast and roll out onto the beach. Agnes drove around in a circle in Golden Gate Park. Ditto in traffic near pier. Agnes found some seaweed." They had heard about the hills in San Francisco but avoided most of them by following the shoreline.

Marie wrote to her brother Albert, "It's always cold in San

Fran at this time of year, they tell us. Everyone was wearing coats all day long. Their warm weather comes in Sept. and Oct. We liked the Pacific at San Fran very much. It was too cold to go swimming, so we just waded. The tide was coming in when we were on the beach—great sport to have the surf rush up."

Zelma wrote in her journal:

> We passed the Bath house and millionaire row with Rudolph Spreckles' home. He is so rich that every blade of grass has a green back and every bird has a bill. His piano has notes and even sense [cents]. Passed Seal Rocks, where the biggest seal was named Taft. Saw Redwood trees, [and] they took a picture of the bus load [in front of a large mirror so we could see how we looked.] At the Presidio Kodaks were put away, because if you took pictures there you would be shot at sunrise. We saw the spot where Pershing's house stood, then passed the Palace of Fine Arts, the only building left from the 1915 World Exposition. We passed the Italian tenements where the bathrooms were on the outside and kids (goat) tied across street— 20,000 Italians. We went to the shipping docks where we had an old-time dinner [for] 40 cents. We went to the Golden Gate Theater for 27 cents, where the ushers wore white gloves.
>
> At Fisherman's Wharf we went to a gift shop, a general store, bought cards and boarded a bus for Chinatown about 8 p.m. Milton had been the guide on the city tour, and we were disappointed that he was not driving [this] bus. At the Ling Ting

Bazaar we saw carved ivory do-dads. We went in one shop where you entered one door and exit[ed] from another. In a basement, we heard Prof. Mon Yuan, 75 years old, entertain on old Chinese musical instruments. The air circulation was not too good, and the air was bad. He played on a flute, a violin, and something that looked like a potato masher with snakeskins. He played "Devil Music" on his guitar for ten cents. Some of us went to a Joss House—lots of incense. Chris and [Bess] had their fortunes told.

When we got back to the terminal, we caught the 10:20 ferry for Berkeley and ran for the Shattock car, arriving [at camp] at about 11:30 p.m.

6. Mountain Vistas

The next day was a traveling day. Marie wanted to make up time, and everyone wanted to get back on schedule for mail. "We left Oakland," Zelma wrote, "[and] caught the car ferry at San Pablo, about six mi. across the Bay, for $1.35 per car. Had a puncture on a little stretch of gravel and went to the courthouse for a comfort station [restroom]. We bought a new tire for $10.95 and had another puncture and bought a new tube for $2.75." At the campsite in Willows the night was so warm they needed no blankets, and Laura wrote, "Marie was hot, but I was just right."

"We came from Willows to Yreka over roads which seemed awful when we went over them the first time," Laura continued. "Swell showers here, and we took advantage of them."

Zelma agreed. "A nice, new campground for 50 cents," she wrote, "with the first hot showers we had found for a while. So I washed my stockings at the same time I took a shower. I must have been driving that day, because I didn't get to bed until 11 p.m."

Yreka, Calif.

Dear Folks:

We're leaving for Crater Lake now and hope to

get there in time to get mail. Gee, but we'll be glad to get out of Calif. Bess is scared she'll get hoof and mouth and foot disease, as she calls it. Yest. we saw a forest fire. S'awful.

Laura.

Marie wrote home, "They are trying to hush up any reports of that disease on account of their fruit crop. If other states forbid shipment, they will be out of luck."

Zelma wrote:

We started early Sun. a.m. in a hot wind and stopped to take pictures of Mt. Shasta. Chris felt out of sorts and told me not to read the signs aloud. So I read them to myself. We had a time finding meat, but bought peaches for 20 cents. Went 65 mi. over red dusty mt. roads until a stretch had been sprinkled, which improved the dustiness. The service station man at Dunsmuir said [when] the Hoof and Mouth inspector at the Cal. border asked us if we had any animals, to tell [him] that we left our husbands at home.

Redding, Cal.
July 20, 1924

Dear Emma,

We are leaving Cal. today, or at least hope to. Have that tough mountain stretch ahead of us now. All's well.

Marie

In a letter to her brother Albert, Marie noted,

We weren't so terribly impressed with the wealth

of California, altho they do disdain pennies. One poor keeper of a camp set up a regular wail when we handed him five pennies." Laura noted that as they passed over the Siskiyou Mountains "Agnes thought our car was burned out, but she really couldn't expect more as we were climbing a steep grade, though it seemed flat on the down grade. We were held up on the boundary of Ore.; a man asked us if we had any animals in our car, and as we didn't he put a sticker on our windshield which announced that we had been *inspected* and *disinfected*. After scaring us by telling us they'd hold our car seven days for fumigation, they let the "Four Iowans" pass.

Zelma wrote:

July 21.

We left early—had oil change (oil 25 cents). We were the second car out of camp. Left Cal. after [driving] thru a solution so tires wouldn't carry "hoof and mouth" disease, [then] coasted down 9 mi. with gas and switch turned off, using brakes only on curves.

We climbed Green Mt. (4800 ft.) cooling our engine twice—once at a spring. Stopped to see Alice Teddy [a trained bear] roller skate. The road from Ashland to Klamath Falls to get to Crater Lake was a beautiful drive between towering pines. There was a lumber camp and pine trees and a recent forest fire area, no park, houses, or towns. We got to Klamath Falls about 1:15. The camp was only 25 cents [for picnicking], but we ate our lunch under a shade tree on the pavement. Gas is still 26 cents, altho it is generally about 35 cents in the mountainous National Parks.

We registered at the Ranger Station for $2.50 for [the] National Park, passed along Anna Canyon Creek, through soft roads, and went up a 10% grade. Gas was low again, and we stopped 50 ft. from the top [to push]. Finally we made it down to the Lodge, where we collected our mail. We saw Crater Lake 1000 feet below. Very deep blue.

"We saw Crater Lake at about 6:59 point 2. Mail from home!" Wrote Laura. Of Crater Lake she remembered, "It was the most vivid blue; you just couldn't believe it could be so blue. There was a mountain crater and a lake in [it], a great big lake—unbelievably blue." But at the time she wrote in her journal, "We froze as there was a very strong, cold wind blowing. Brrr!!!"

∽

On a cloudy March day, Rob and I packed shovels and drove into the mountains, up a winding road thick with heavy snow and truck-wide ruts, to dig down and see our dirt. We owned ten acres in Montana with no covenants. Neither of us had a job or any money—we weren't even married yet—but we borrowed the deposit from Grandma Marie and bought the land anyway. We could be artists there. Some day we could build a studio and have a photo business near our home on our land. At age twenty-two it didn't occur to us that no customer would drive up there for photography.

In midsummer, the season of fast lushness and cows in the mountains, we bought a condemned married-student house for $300 and moved it. We took pictures of it traveling down the middle of Main Street, argued with the hauler over where to set it down, and lost. Had the fence line been accurate, it would have touched the back door.

We called it our shack-toe. At first the house sat on railroad ties, its asbestos siding slipped and cracked, the roofline as crooked as the high ridge behind it. We cemented some poles in the ground and set the house on crossbeams cut from the woods and planed flat on two sides with a chainsaw. Then we moved in. No water, no power, no phone, no skirting, and what passed for insulation in only the lower three feet of the thin walls.

We got a hairy white dog and named him Bones. Someone gave us an old mattress rather than haul it to the dump. We bought a Coleman camp stove and set it in the kitchen. At bedtime we gathered our shoes by the bed. When mice thumped in the walls (they didn't rustle), we threw a shoe at the sound. If we were lucky we fell asleep before they moved again.

The road we lived on was notorious. Even four-wheel drives sometimes got stuck. Back when the coal mines were in operation, workers had spread black coke dust over the road, thinking it would help the thick clay dry quicker. But when it got wet, the dust congealed into a layer of black slime, slippery as oil, and we were thankful for the deep mud ruts that kept us from spinning off the edge.

Winter came, and the constant wind up the valley varied from breeze to gale and blew right under the house, up through the floor, and through the plywood walls. Our driveway drifted in with the first heavy December snow, and until May we walked the last 150 yards. It was just as well we had no plumbing, for when we got home from work the temperature was the same outside and inside, our quick fire giving only token heat in the dark before we crawled under a mound of blankets, knit hats still on.

∽

Crater Lake, Ore.
July 22, 1924

Dear Albert,

Well, we arrived at this place [Crater Lake] yesterday. The lake is a beautiful sight. We are perched on the rim looking down about 1000 feet to the water's edge. It's about six miles across and is about 2000 ft. deep in some places. The sides of the rim are quite steep and varicolored. The waters are a deep indigo blue with rose and purple etc. colored reflections from the sides. Lots of pines up here where we are. We are sitting in the sun as it's too cold in the shade. Had to move our breakfast table out into the sunlight this morning.

You can't imagine water looking as blue as this lake is.

The roads leading up to this place were very good. Don't think we'll hit anything quite as tough as the Sierras leading into Yosemite. Understand we have paving into Mt. Rainier Nat. Park.

We got our mail yesterday, three letters from home forwarded from the Yosemite. Those rubes go over the mail so fast they overlook half one's mail. I'm sure those letters were in Yosemite when we were there. Didn't get any addressed to this place, however. Will call for our mail again this p.m.

Our flivver is working great now. Had to have a

new timer as she wasn't pulling as of yore. Surely hit a stretch of bad luck in Yosemite. People as a rule treat us fine. Last nite, the kids had a hard time finding wood. First thing we knew a couple drove up to our camp and unloaded a big pile for our use. Said they saw we were in need so had just driven out into the forest and collected some for us.

We hiked down to the lake this afternoon. 'Twas worse going down than coming up—not bad though. When we got back, we got our mail—a whole lot they have been storing for some time, I imagine.

Those two New York fellows that we met clear back in Colorado drove into camp a little while ago. Guess we were as tickled as they were. Seems just like meeting life long acquaintances.

Well, must close now as it's late and getting mighty chilly.

Marie.

Laura wrote in her journal, "We slept late and I made breakfast, therefore a late breakfast [9:45]. We climbed down to the water's edge, and Agnes and Bess went [around it] in a boat. Of course they said it was wonderful, but it cost them $3.00, so we were feeling fine." Zelma wrote, "We walked down to the edge of the Lake. It only took about 20 minutes down a winding path. But when we tried to climb back, it took us 1½ hours. A sand storm came up, and we had to wash our dishes twice. We ate our dinner in a tent."

Laura noted, "We saw our friends from NY, and Grace and I entertained them around the campfire while the rest went to hear a concert." A ranger from Kansas was supposed to sing, but the concert was canceled because it was too windy. "That night the wind came up again and we nearly froze," wrote Zelma. "[It was] so cold we wore flannel pj's, bed sox, sweater and bathrobe." It was the only time the canvas water bottle for the radiator, which they carried outside the car, froze solid.

They left Crater Lake the following morning, wrapped in coats and blankets. Laura wrote in her journal, "We looked for 'NY' and 'Ohio' but couldn't find their camp. Later we saw them on the road." Zelma noted that the drive to Medford was beautiful. "Saw a big forest fire," she wrote. "The kids left me at a gas station, and I had to walk seven blocks before I found the others."

At Salem the cars split up. Marie noted that while "the other bunch went on to Portland," her car wanted to visit some "people from Decorah that Grace and Agnes knew." So while Ophelia camped at Salem, Jenny continued on to Myrtle Creek and Silverton. They planned to reunite at Kelso, Washington, in two days.

[postmarked Myrtle Creek, Ore., July 24]

Dear Mother:

We're planning on getting to Silverton today— 200 miles abt. Everything is fine, but all the kids are kind of thinking of home.

Crater Lake was surely beautiful. Agnes and Bess could not enjoy it enough on land, so they took to the water. We enjoyed ourselves as much as they.

Yest. we saw what a store man called a very bad forest fire. We weren't close at all.

Laura

In her journal Laura wrote, "We spent a very enjoyable evening at the home of C. E. Jorgenson. It surely seemed nice to talk Norwegian again—to real Norwegians. We slept on real beds for a night [and] saw real holly. Agnes, Grace, Bianca and Helga entertained us at the piano." Marie added, "They were tickled to see us."

Meanwhile, the other kids washed their clothes at the Salem campground and then saw a double-feature movie. The next day they toured Portland, where Zelma had her "neck clipped" and noted, "Lost in Chinatown. Bess and [Martha] leave us at PO, and [Martha] gets lost and doesn't return for four hours and 20 minutes." On their way to Kelso the following morning, Zelma noted, "35 cent toll to get to Vancouver revolving bridge. Eat lunch at 2:30." Jenny also headed out, and Laura wrote, "On to Kelso, where we had an awful time finding Zelma's aunt. They visited our camp bringing eats." Zelma noted that after providing cherries and pie, her Aunt Julia, Uncle Will and cousin John took them to a "banjo logrolling contest."

The next day Marie wrote home, "Hope to make Mt. Rainier today. Have cloudy weather—the first since we left Nebraska." Laura wrote, "At Tacoma Grace and Agnes left their knickers to have them cleaned. In the course of their search for a laundry they talked to a real "chink" who said "tellee, craeke, etc." It seemed as if there were an awful lot of big cities in Wash. We got a very bad impression of [the state] as it was a cold, foggy day and Agnes and I froze almost all forenoon. We wished that we had our coats out of the pack. We'd never live in Wash!"

They reached Tacoma Park at suppertime and paid the $2.50 entrance fee. In her journal Laura noted that they "arrived at Longmire Springs in a little while." There they camped, and she added, "No letters from home."

Longmire Springs, Rainier Natl. Park
July 27, 1924

Dear Folks,

We called for mail last nite and there was none for me at all. Marie neither. Agnes and Martha either. Gee! We're going up to Paradise valley this morning. It's foggy here but it's s'posed to be clear there. Marie and I were very comfortable last nite but Agnes and Grace say they froze. We are planning on getting to Seattle tomorrow, but we'll very likely not make it. Love from

Laura

In her journal Laura added:

July 27

We slept late, had our breakfast (pancakes) and went up to Paradise Valley. The road for a ways was only one way and was very good in all places. It was not especially good for "nerves," however. We got only one peek at Mt. Rainier as the clouds were hanging so low. That look was surely worth a lot, though, it was the grandest sight we'd seen. We also hiked up so far that we could see the Nisqually Glacier. We had dinner [noon] near Paradise Inn, and after that I nearly froze to death while waiting for the kids to come back to the car.

On the way down to camp from Paradise Valley we hiked to see the place where the Nisqually River emerges from beneath the glacier. The ice rose to a height of about 60 feet (very dirty). The river itself was of a dirty color, being full of silt.

Huge boulders could be heard crashing into one another as they were forced along by the rush of the stream.

Laura remembered the glacier later, in an interview: "I remember how we walked up to the tip of the glacier, to that great big cliff of ice above us, and the water came rolling out from underneath, rolling the boulders as it came. A cliff of ice . . ." She trailed off into thought. Zelma noted that they "climbed onto the Nisqually Glacier. We found a board, and I have a picture of us sliding down the glacier on a board [in July]."

In the blanks of a prewritten postcard, called a "Travelogue," Marie also wrote home; "[Mount Rainier is] great when the clouds don't hide it. They cleared for about 5 min. yest. We hiked up to the snow banks yesterday—also had a fine view of a glacier." Then she noted in the margin, "We are leaving for Seattle today—rite on schedule. We didn't get any mail here at all." But of the park Marie remembered only Mt. Rainier, standing snowcapped and alone, its base almost at sea level with the peak rising nearly three miles to 14,410 feet. "Mt. Rainier," she said in interview, awe in her voice almost seventy years later; "that was a gorgeous thing. Gee it was impressive."

"July 28: We got up very late and went on to Seattle." Laura wrote in her journal, "Of course Agnes had to make some remark about how well our tires were holding out, so we had a leak and a blowout on our way. The other kids sailed past us as if they owned the elements. When we were just within the city limits of Seattle we had a sweet little blowout about three inches in diameter. As we had no extra, we drove in on our flat tire—tuf!" Zelma wrote, "We lost a pillow on the way to [Seattle, where we] found a camp with showers and a shampoo." Jenny Pep got to camp late, as they'd stopped to visit some friends, Clara and Etta. "After supper," Laura wrote, "we saw slides of Washington and heard a very interesting talk by good looking U. of Wash. guy. When we got bored we looked at him and felt greatly refreshed." The next day she continued, "Up early and off for a tour of the city."

Marie noted, "[Dr. Jepson, a friend of Martha's] came up [and] took all eight of us all over Seattle to see the sights. We saw the U. of W., the government locks in operation, had a swim at the beach, etc. etc. He sure treated us royally." He insisted they must take a boat to Vancouver. After traveling so far, it was unthinkable not to.

Zelma wrote that in touring Seattle "[We] got on the Rainier car and went too far and had to transfer." The only thing Grace remembered of Seattle was visiting her cousin, who was in the service at that time. "He invited me out to a Chinese dinner for the evening," she said, "and suggested going in that there was a restroom. But I was too bashful to go. So by the time we got back to camp I really had troubles!"

Laura wrote in her journal, "July 29: Had dinner [noon] at 'Eagle Cafe,' we four eating in one booth, the dolls in another. In the evening we went to Clara's for supper and met [her friends] Hans and Grant and also Hugo Bode. Hans was rather sophisticated and showed us the latest in tango. 'Rural summers' formed a delightful conversation topic. Hans and Grant took us through the main streets by night, to show us where they'd worked mostly. When we got back to camp we talked until the cop came to tell us to be quiet (Grace still later)." Marie noted, "Had a fine time—danced 'n everything."

The next day Laura wrote in her journal, "July 30: We lay around camp all day while the rest of the kids (except Marie, Grace and me) went to Victoria (spent more cash)." Although they did want to go, Marie and Laura were running short of money, with the whole West between them and home.

Zelma wrote, "Next day we took a steamer, 'Princess Victoria,' to Victoria. The sea was rough. We saw salmon, forts, battle ships, and gulls. At Victoria was Canadian stamps and money. Pop. 40,000, 5,000 of which are Chinese. [We took] a rubberneck wagon [tour and] saw Old English Gardens (Bouchard), custom office, Parliament Bldg., statue of Victoria. The Princess Hotel rates were 25 and up—mostly up."

After washing clothes all day, Laura noted, "In the evening we spoke to a lady who used to live [near Decorah] in Winneshiek County. We also spoke to three diabolical creatures who roused the curiosity of the camp. In the course of the evening we went over in the clubhouse to watch them dance, and the good-looking U. of Wash. guy asked me to dance!!*&$#%@!! We went to bed and sleep waiting for the kids to show up."

Throughout my life I visited Grandma Marie whenever I had time, money, and inclination all at once. Every three years a family reunion was held, where the fate of the Brick House was debated, and I attended as many of those as I could. But I preferred a three-day visit by myself. Sometimes I drove, sometimes I flew, and often I rode the bus, at least for the final leg. I liked looking out the window and watching brilliant green roll past as my creative juices stirred. I liked that Greyhound stopped for Amish buggies parked along the highway, to pick up or drop off gentle bearded or bonneted bus riders from another time.

Once I came south from Minnesota through an evening thunderstorm. When day turned to night was impossible to tell, for the world was totally black outside the bus lights. A torrential downpour washed like waves over a boat, and brilliant lightning grounded and cracked, wicking draft horses and corn tassels white as Grandpa's hair.

I later heard that after three days fish and relatives smell, but for me that was long enough to climb the bluff, to take Laura out for a strawberry milkshake, and to bring Grandma Marie to church. After she stopped driving I always stayed over a Sunday. Though in my regular life I didn't attend church, I gained respect for taking time out of every week to step from daily thinking and look at a bigger picture. I could understand why it fed her. But after three days I was regenerated, talked out, and ready to go home. Whether my presence was old to Grandma Marie I don't know.

One Christmas holiday my husband Rob and I went to Iowa. Grandma Marie had been sick the previous October—was even hospitalized briefly—but pulled through. I wanted to visit her then but couldn't arrange it. Once she was sent home, I mailed herbal teas, colorful plastic flowers, the book *Letters of a Woman Homesteader*, her favorite sardines, and the lentil beans she liked to sprout. No homemade cookies because of her poor health. But I really wanted to see her and could finally get away for Christmas.

Grandma Marie's birthday was two days after Christmas, and my husband and I planned to brighten her holiday, her birthday, and the long dark winter that is so hard on old people, especially those living alone. Everyone else in the family was coming to her ninetieth birthday party the following year, and that celebration was already being organized, but I thought that eighty-nine was pretty darn old too.

Rob and I planned a traditional Norwegian lutefisk and lefse dinner for Christmas Eve and invited Grandma Marie's younger sister, Laura. No one else wanted to eat lutefisk, the notoriously horrid lye-soaked fish revered by stoic old-timers. Grandma Marie and Laura were touched that we would even consider serving it to them, and when I picked Laura up she was bubbling with excitement. "Better than pizza and Snickers!" she exclaimed.

They lived across town from each other and talked on the phone every day, but they rarely saw each other because neither could drive anymore.

Lucky for us, it was a good year for lutefisk; it was a mild batch with a texture similar to sushi. But even more stunning than decent lutefisk were Laura and Grandma Marie. We watched in amazement as they wrapped huge gobs of dripping white meat in the tortilla-like lefse and slurped it all down. I had never seen them eat with such abandon, elbows on the shaky table, juice dripping down their jowls. They talked and smacked their lips and laughed freely.

Marie must have noticed our open mouths. "This is a treat for us," she explained. "As children we always had lutefisk and lefse for Christmas."

Every Christmas Eve they climbed the snow-fringed bluffs framing their home and cut a tree. It could be tall because the drawing room ceiling was high, and it could be beautiful because it was free. While their father built a Yule fire in the smoky fireplace (normally only the kitchen had heat), the children admired the box of glass ornaments and metal candle holders, running their fingers gently over the colorful textures. When their mother brought out her gifts—mittens and hats she'd knitted throughout the year, wrapped in reused paper—the children rushed off to gather their own hidden presents. Every fall their mother gave each child a bit of her "turkey money" to buy a small gift for each of the others. It was the only time gifts were exchanged.

Once the presents were gathered, their father shooed everyone from the drawing room and shut the door on them. No children allowed while the tree was trimmed. The sun set, and the cold and dark thickened around the Brick House, but the children could hear their father singing Christmas carols and Norwegian hymns while their mother carefully rolled out potato dough as thin as possible. She heated the large, flat lefse on the griddle until thin bubbles came up and browned, then stacked them under a dishtowel.

The children helped cook or played together, always with one eye on the drawing room door, memorizing the design of the doorknob, the texture of the wood, the small kite traced in the paint. Laura did that once as they played hide-and-go-seek while their mother painted the kitchen door. Instead of covering her eyes while she counted, young Laura drew a kite in the wet paint with her finger, and it was still there years later.

By the time the dishtowel was steaming and tall with tender lefse, the door cracked open. "Samle barna!" their father bellowed: gather the children. Then he flung the door wide. In a billowing scent of fresh-cut evergreens, before the glimmering Yule embers, stood their sparkling, candlelit Christmas tree.

Star-struck, they paused in the doorway, then poured in and opened their gifts: a set of jacks, a deck of cards, a drawing pad, a book, mittens. If they were lucky, their father danced. He did a Norwegian men's stomping dance that culminated with him whirling around and around the room, gathering enough momentum to kick toward the ceiling. Then they joked about whether his own father actually did kick the ceiling in Norway and guessed how high or low it must have been, and finally they ate lutefisk and lefse.

"It was the only time we had it all year," Laura noted, wiping her chin with her wrist.

"Usually we had the same things every day," Marie added. "In those days women didn't have to rack their brains to think of different meals all the time." For breakfast it was toast and milk, for dinner it was salted pork and potatoes, and for supper it was substantial quantities of grot. This was not the rich Norwegian butter pudding called rommegrot but a mush made from course graham flour and hot water. "We were poor and couldn't afford much, but our mother raised seven strapping boys on that good whole-grain cereal," Marie said. "It was a part of the day." She told me that once when unexpected guests arrived for supper, their mother butchered chickens and served a nicer meal. But at bedtime a cry came from the children. "We can't go to bed yet! We haven't had our grot!"

Laura's eyes glittered, and her deep laugh filled the kitchen. "That's why we liked lutefisk," she said. "It was something different."

The morning after her birthday I found Grandma Marie stuffing bedsheets down the laundry chute under her kitchen sink. "I've run out of sheets," she said with a sideways look. I knew at once I'd woken too early and caught her red-handed. Her washer and dryer were in the basement, and my Uncle Bill and cousin Greg had warned me that she was weaker now and not allowed in the basement. The stairs were steep and dark, and the floor below was concrete. They didn't want her to fall.

"I'll wash them for you," I offered.

"You're the guest!" she replied, "I can't let you do that. And besides, you don't know how the washer works." Before I knew it she made a shuffling spring for the stairs. She was thinner and shorter than before her illness, more stooped but just as determined, and quicker.

I had my own quandary. If she wanted to do her laundry in the basement at age eighty-nine, shouldn't she get to? Myself, I'd rather die falling down the stairs than sitting in a chair. "I'm not supposed to go down here, you know," she called back to me. "They say it's too dangerous." Her laughter decided me. I followed her down the creaking steps, gray boards as old as she was, and no handrail.

The brand-new washer and dryer stood on the south wall, but Grandma Marie didn't go toward them. With some sort of unspoken understanding I held back, watching, as she pulled a washtub on legs and an old-fashioned wringer washer out of the shadows.

"What about the new washer?" I asked.

"Don't know how it works," she answered, dragging out another washtub.

"I can show you."

"I won't remember. Greg's showed me lots of times." She set the third tub in place and turned on the hot water. She looked at me. "I've used this all my life."

As the washer filled, bubbling and steamy, she hauled the basket of sheets over. "There's always an order to doing the laundry this way," she said. "First the whites, then the colors, and last the overalls. By then the water is cold. Sometimes, growing up with all those boys, the wash water got too dirty and we had to wash the overalls in the first-rinse water."

She stretched out the sheets one by one and added them to

the churning, foamy water. "We got our soft water from the rain barrel back then," she mused. "It was as big around as my kitchen table. We caught rain from the roof and heated it on the stove. The whites were washed in boiling water." She tugged at the pile of remaining dirty sheets, freeing them up for the next batch.

"Even in the winter we'd hang everything out on the line," she said. "It froze solid, of course, but that was the first step in drying." Then she showed me how to feed the sheets into the wringer one after the next, a braid of sheets falling into the steaming first rinse, then the second, and finally into the original basket. "Not too thick," she said, "just so."

The water cooled and grayed gradually as her liver-spotted hands pulled tangle after tangle of soaking fabric into a consistent weave while she talked. The dim corners of the basement seemed to draw away from us as her mind ranged. She told me about one of her third-grade students during the Depression. "She didn't have any decent shoes," Grandma Marie said, "let alone overshoes for the snow." As the weather got colder the little girl came to school nearly barefooted, her shoes were so worn. Grandma Marie was a teacher and had a paying job when many didn't, and she couldn't bear the idea of a child out in the snow like that. One day she asked the girl's mother for permission to buy her some shoes. "It wasn't something you just went out and did," Grandma Marie said. "People had their pride, and if that was all they had . . . " she shrugged. But this mother embraced her and said yes and thank you. So Grandma Marie took the little girl downtown and bought her shoes and, on impulse, overshoes as well. "Shoes are very important to little children," she told me, pressing a damp sheet back into the overflowing basket.

"I got a letter from her the other day," Grandma Marie continued.

"From the little girl?"

"Yes. Of course she's an old lady now too. But she found
me and wrote to me to say thank you for those shoes. After
all these years she still remembered it." Then, looking up at
the pipes that ran across the ceiling, "I guess we can hang the
sheets down here to dry. Usually I don't have so many." It was
her only moment of indecision.

"We could use the dryer," I said. "I know how it works."

She thought for a moment, looking at the shiny machine. I
suddenly realized that she kept it dusted. "All right," she said,
and hefted the basket over to it. She peered at the buttons
and dials. "I just can't fathom it all," she said. "You young
people just pick up on these things. My old mind can't get
around it."

While the dryer hummed, we drained and wiped out the
washtubs, letting the water out through short hoses from
their uncorked drains to run across the floor and into the
floor drain. One of the hoses was clogged. "Billy tried to fix
that for me," Grandma Marie noted. With a wire snake and
a lot of shared stubbornness and persistence the two of us
freed the clog and giggled that we weren't even engineers. By
then the dryer buzzed, making Grandma Marie jump. She
pulled out a streaming pile of warm white sheets, leaning
back from the sheer bulk, and headed toward the stairs. I
wondered how she could even lift them and knew her plan
was to iron them all.

I followed her closely up the stairs. About halfway up she
paused and smiled over her shoulder, "You're here to catch
me, aren't you."

When Rob and I left for home, Grandma Marie stood on her back steps. She balanced herself on the icy sidewalk with one hand on her silver-handled cane. We didn't see her turn and go inside, only her standing frail and white-haired and waving—as she always did, because her mother always had.

Shortly afterward Billy and Greg fixed the basement door. The next time Grandma Marie tried to use it the doorknob fell off, but the door remained locked (some things engineers can do). Because she wasn't supposed to go down there she couldn't ask to have it fixed, and nothing was ever said about the dangling knob.

∽

They started for home on August 1, heading east after seven weeks on the road. Laura's journal reads:

> *July 31*
>
> We passed through the queerest country this day—desert along side of prosperous orchards. Stopped at Snoqualmie Falls, which were a minus quality [dry]. At Wenatchee we thought the kids were behind [when] they were ahead of us, camping at the City camp in the same town. We waited and waited for them and finally they came to look for us. S'awful. We camped in an orchard, listening to crickets all night.

> *August 1*
>
> The kids came down to our camp for breakfast, and we discovered [their] imagination had been spoofed by [the] camp manager. To ease his conscience he gave us almost all the stickers he had. We passed through "Great Coulee" [before the

dam]; a place where a glacier had passed through years ago. [There] we had a little debate about *The White Sister* [movie]. Grace vs. The Rest of Us! [Here she drew a picture of a woman in a hat with a down-turned mouth, saying "Fooie" and labeled "Grace."] Drove through wheat fields all afternoon and camped at Spokane, down in a ditch.

Zelma wrote, "We saw great wheat fields before we got to Spokane." The golden fields curved endlessly to the horizon, like monstrous ocean swells. Marie thought this must be what it looked like in Alberta, where brother Sig's family lived, and where all they could grow was wheat. Laura wrote in her journal, "We had our leaky radiator fixed in Spokane." To her folks she wrote, "Just a few lines to let you know that I think this card will beat the card I wrote yest. We got to Spokane last night. Roads were like washboards and had loose gravel on them. Marie drove. We haven't got any mail from home since Crater Lake and it was addressed to Yosemite. '?' Well, there's nothing to write, and since I've written it I might as well close." She also noted, "One of the girls had greetings to bring to a Mr. Axberg. So she called him up, and he came down to camp. He was one of the three greatest American aviators in the World War. We are more important than you thot we were, Emma!"

"Next day we were in three states," Zelma noted. "We left Washington, ate lunch at Coeur d'Alene [Idaho], and camped at Superior, Montana." Laura continued, "On our way to Superior we passed through vast areas of burned timber. At a sawmill, or rather a planing mill, a man told us the forests had burned in 1910—the time I figured Sigurd was out here. We camped at Superior and had supper after the kids got in, which they finally did—on their rim. They ruined sed rim." Zelma noted in her journal that a "Camel's hump" ruined their rim, and they had to wait "for man to eat supper, read paper and smoke pipe" before he'd fix their car.

Laura continued, "After supper we went to a real western dance and had a dandy time. Chris surely did get the men. Between dances out in Montana they promenade around the hall." Zelma noted, "music all night."

Marie sent a postcard to her young nephew, John. It was postmarked in Missoula and read, "We came here just now. Traveling over mt. roads all along. Marie," but the picture on the other side was a cartoon of a laughing donkey.

7. Galloping Bare-Breasted

Laura's journal reads:

August 5 (Sun)

Passed through Missoula. On a rather high grade a car had gone off the road, turned over completely and landed on its wheels. Only one lady slightly hurt. A nice little tack on the road found refuge in our tire, so we changed to one with a slow leak and I had to jump out at intervals to pump it up. At Deer Lodge we had our tire fixed and the repairman told us all about a Roundup to be held at Bozeman, August 7, 8 and 9. We all decided to go the 9th after going through Yellowstone in a hurry.

At Deer Lodge, Zelma wrote; "Martha's cousin got permission for us to go thru the [state] prison. It was a scary feeling to hear the big gate click behind us. We wondered if they would let us out!" Laura wrote, "Remember we got [teaching] application blanks from here [Deer Lodge], Emma? Would have been great place." In her journal she added, "We visited the Montana Pen and had lots of fun listening to our clever guide. [He] had a loose tooth that [slipped] out of place. A special detachment of four guards was used to watch us so as we wouldn't wink at any good looking prisoners."

They continued on to Anaconda, known for its copper mines, where Laura wrote, "[Got] off the road into a bug house. We were shown through the copper smelters by a nut who had the giggles." But Grace had a different memory of the copper smelters. "[We were] looking in on those terrible, hot fiery furnaces," she said, "and [the tour guide] said if you pick up a [shiny] piece of copper [from] the floor, you can see what you're going to look like in eternity," she laughed. "Here we were facing those hot fiery furnaces."

Laura noted in her journal, "We got as far as Three Forks, where we camped at a punk camp with rotten accommodations; free, however." Zelma wrote, "We crossed the continental divide and lost our radiator cap for the first time."

The next day they continued through Bozeman to Livingston and on to Yellowstone Park. They followed the massive blue Yellowstone River through a valley bordered on the east by the even more massive, and aptly named, Beartooth-Absaroka Mountains. Marie noted, "The roads to and around the Yellowstone were a prairie compared to the ones leading into [Yosemite]," though Zelma noted it was "a poor narrow road."

In a letter to Emma, Laura wrote, "We just got here and I am sitting outside 'Mammoth Hot Springs Inn' while Marie, Grace and Agnes go in to get the mail. We didn't get any at either Rainier or Seattle so are surely expecting some today. A few of the girls are expecting money. *I'm* not!"

They did have mail, but no checks at first. "Gee, tears were shed when the girls didn't get their cash," wrote Laura. "One letter from Emma. Gee, [it was] fine!" Emma's letter was for-

Galloping Bare-Breasted

warded from general delivery in Seattle to Yellowstone. Laura replied immediately.

Yellowstone Natl. Park
Aug. 5, 1924

Dear Emma,

Yas, I got your letter also one from Thelma Ramsey. I got one from Ella Johnson and you this morning, so I feel pretty good. Marie got one from Herman so she feels pretty nice too. We are passing out of this park Fri., then we plan to go straight to Bozeman, camp there and take in their roundup the next day. We're all crazy to go to one.

We're all draped around a blistering hot fire waiting for bears to show up. Ag. just fired a stick at the fire and a part hit Bess, whereupon Bess yelled, "Laura, quit throwing things at me, Agnes." S'awful! They all pick on me! [Martha] asked Christy today if her niece was a boy. Gee, these kids—they don't think! [They] are *writing letters* and *talking about rangers*! Agnes just got thru sploshing soapy water on my shoes, so now it's my turn to wash.

The kids are getting ready for bed now. Bess and Christy took [heated] stones wrapped in paper, and Bess caught fire. Marie's been talking abt. bears all day. Here's where we dream.

Well Emma, Pa, Ma, Ahhlbert, Walter and John, I find it necessary to repair to my marcel bed—uff! You may notice that I'm not hitting these lines. I just noticed it. You c its getting dark as the fire is dying! Yas!

How is Ma? I hope she isn't going to have those spells again. Well I really can't think of anything more to write so I mite as well close. We're all well and going fine. Had a blowout in our last original fabric today. Pretty good! Eh? [drawing of smiling girl]

Goodbi, Laura.

❧

Rob and I liked feeling wild and tough in our mountain home at first, but at some point all the splitting wood, moving snow, digging out the car, hauling water, and construction turned from challenges into chores. After seven years we welcomed phone lines and gradually gained power, water, and insulation. We ripped out the interior walls and drew new floor plans, but remodeling came slowly.

I worked nights and spent days on the mountain. I broke out my cross-country skis early in the season, when the fences still showed, and Bones and I packed down my three favorite loops—the wind-protected ones, thick with creaking pines and curving hills steep enough to warm my toes on the way up but not scare me coming down. The trails looped off each other over fences, sagebrush, and ridges. The longest one took all afternoon, with views of mountain ranges in every direction.

I skied every day to keep my trails open in spite of fresh snow and blowing drifts. I started out feeling underdressed, the chill cutting through sweater and gloves. But working up the first hill I warmed up, breathing into a scarf, my glasses frosted at first and then defogged by my own breath. I skied in brilliant subzero sun, in shirtsleeves sun, in blustering wind and pelting snow, and in sparkling moonlight. One evening I skied into a violet sky and a hanging cloud.

Galloping Bare-Breasted

Fresh snow buffered the icy trail and stuck to the sides of tree trunks. I took the middle trail, a puff of breath and my ski tips emerging at every step, until the purple diffused into white, and air and earth fogged together without seam or shadow. In knee-deep snow my muscles told me I was moving upward, but my eyes strained for contour, for a focal point. I turned my ski tips toward what I knew was downhill and felt myself slip over the icy earth, my legs adjusting blindly to a fast-moving, hidden terrain, but I could see no motion. Caught in an all-white world, parallel lines stretching behind, I flew into infinity.

On a clear September day Rob rode his motorcycle up the road, stopping here and there to photograph flares of yellow aspens. One moment he was riding along looking at the trees, the next he was trying to kick-start a damaged bike as blood ran from his temple. He survived a concussion from the accident, but the damage to his shoulders and upper back was permanent.

The long, cold, sometimes impossible commute became intolerable. Some days he came home unable to lift his arms. How he could steer on that jouncing, numbing drive I never knew. He worked late, in part to avoid our home with all its looming projects. He called before he left town, and I ran a hot bath in the six-foot claw-foot tub we had hauled up from the creek, timed to empty the water heater just as he walked in.

I still wanted us to share our adventures and chores in the mountain wildness, but Rob plain couldn't do it anymore. He couldn't dig the Scout out of the snow, couldn't split wood, couldn't haul groceries and dog food from the road on a sled. He threw his energies into his photo business in town. I stoked the fire, did the daily chores, wrote poetry, and skied alone. Then we decided to start a family. It wasn't a sudden thing but a gradual longing that welled in us. Perhaps this was a dream we could share.

I stopped waitressing when I started knocking drinks over with my belly. It felt good to lie by the wood stove and wait for the baby. Through the sunny part of fall, before the real cold and snow, I teetered around on long, skinny legs, a circus tent out front. I cooked beans, baked pies and cookies, sewed a bright baby quilt, watched the weather and the seven whitetails in our aspen trees, and waited. Rob hired help to finish the new concrete foundation and lowered our house onto it. Then he started putting up sheet rock.

After twelve years it was still very much our shack-toe, with sheets for walls and unfinished, splintery floors. The midwife was dubious. She said we could birth there only if the roads were dry. My mother was terrified, forgetting that she herself had been born on a farm. A week before the due date she called from California. "So where are you going to have this baby?" she demanded. For the hundredth time I explained my philosophy that birth and death are part of living and hospitals an unnecessary alienation. That it would take thirty minutes to assemble an emergency team at the hospital, and we could be there by then. That after twenty years of running, I trusted my body. I didn't understand her concern. It all made perfect sense to me.

The November day our son was born it was fifty-one degrees and sunny. The road was dry. This is always the first detail relayed. Only seconds old, he stopped crying the instant I spoke, wobbling his head and bright eyes toward me. He slept in the warmth between Rob and me, his pink nose and sweet breath emerging from under a white knit cap. We answered his contented little grunts with our own. Two weeks later we named him Robert Max, Max for short. Mom admitted bragging to her friends that we birthed at home. Now that she wasn't afraid for us, she could feel proud.

My life blurred into feeding, diapering, cooking, diapering, cleaning and feeding and diapering. Days disappeared without a moment to spare, but nothing got done. I didn't answer the phone and started the daily argument during morning nap: dishes or writing? Every midafternoon I felt the chill rush when the sun slipped behind the ridge and I realized I'd been inside all day again. I'd bundle Max into the front carrier and hurry down the driveway, chasing the receding sunlight.

We often crossed the road and slipped through the barbed wire gate into the horse pasture. My favorite, the brown mare, had a new golden colt. Her strong body was soft around the edges and saggy like mine, her stance protective. "Your son is beautiful," I'd say, or "Don't worry, you'll get your figure back." I would have invited her to tea if I could, to chat together while our golden-haired sons played. Instead I stood in knee-deep snow and talked to a horse.

At night I could ski while Rob watched Max. Bones's eyes lit up when he sensed my gear, but he was too old and crippled-up to manage deep snow. I left him thumping his tail in anguish as I skied away from the rim of light and warmth. I could feel the ski trail through snow and skis, but I never saw it, only an endless black depth of cold sky swathed with an orgasm of stars, like the breath frozen on my scarf. Then the lion came. We saw her big tracks. Our neighbor saw her, then backtracked to find she'd trailed him for miles. Curious? Stalking? I stopped skiing at night. A running motion, like cross-country skiing, triggers a lion's instinct to pounce.

Some days I drove seven miles to the highway to pick up the mail, just to get out of the house. Some days I never did get out but watched from the window. A black moose hung like a shadow deep in the winter trees. Wind picked up wood chips as big as my hand and flung them into the sky.

I buried Bones on his favorite lookout point. The full moon was setting in a clear predawn winter sky. All the coyotes in the hills around our shack-toe burst into warbling howls as I chipped frozen sod to cover him.

One winter night I dreamed I was ten years old, galloping my pony through the tall summer grass with my friend Cindy. We wore cut-off shorts and pixie haircuts, and our knees clung to the ponies' fat sides, feet splayed for balance in a way no one ever taught us, no book ever described. Cindy looked back at me and smiled, and as I watched, her face, her smile, became the most beautiful thing I'd ever seen.

When I awoke, the memories were as vivid as the dream; Cindy and Misty, me and Beauty. One afternoon Misty was mad. Every time we climbed on, she bucked us off. We thought it was funny until the next morning when Misty had a new golden colt and three of the big sows that shared her pasture were found kicked to death.

I lay awake in the mountains and imagined details I never thought about when I was ten. A golden foal pushed into new darkness, sliding from a heaving, sweaty mare. Kicking free of slippery membranes with awkward long legs, it snorts a first searing breath, the air alive with blood scent, ravenous grunting, and striking hooves.

Time passed. Life flowed into Max's limbs. He rolled over, sat up, and crawled, exploring his world equally with hands, feet, and tongue. He slept in a backpack as I dug wildflower bulbs from the horse pasture and the golden colt frisked around his sturdy mother. While Max learned to tuck his face into a scarf and hang on when I pulled him in a sled behind my skis, the golden colt was weaned, gelded, and returned to the horse pasture.

Workers put gravel down on the road, and the mud swallowed it up. They laid pit run, rocks bigger than my two fists, then more gravel. Houses replaced cows along the road, slowly at first, then furiously. The horse pasture was divided and fenced, a road cut through it and framed with real estate signs. Suddenly our land had value. We got a lien and moved to town.

Friends thought it was because of Max, or for him, but it wasn't that. Rob's business was flourishing, but it kept him away too much. What if we could really have it by our home? A finished home without an exhausting commute? I wanted a real cupboard or closet, a floor that wasn't patched with duct tape, a house where my bedroom wasn't filled with construction supplies and my bed wasn't in the living room. I looked at the carcass of my dream, white sinew and bone exposed, and took the bloody heart.

Rob and I found a place in town bordered by two unkempt parks and a creek, with a lot big enough for wild edges, for garden and weeds. Our street was originally a buffalo trail. Six blocks from Main Street, foxes killed our chickens. In the spring, ancient lilacs and tulips burst forth without prompting, and the fruit trees we planted survived. The house itself was old, big, and mostly empty of furniture. After three days, two-year-old Max announced he was no longer afraid of the furnace fans.

We ripped out the shag carpeting, fixed the porch, grew attached to the orange kitchen countertops. But we also cut up the original half-planed shack-toe foundation beams and set them in the ground for a sandbox. We gutted the bathroom to add a long claw-foot bathtub like the one we had in the mountains. This tub wasn't pulled from the creek bed, its clawed feet strewn among the rushes, but it gave a good bath.

I missed parts of living in the mountains, missed knowing the land and weather as well as my own moods. I missed the sense of belonging like wildlife to the familiar landscape, missed the skiing, even as variable as it became. Still, I didn't regret selling the house that we finished after we moved out. A younger me could never have believed the flood rush of dreams could be directed, conjured, but now I painted the floor in my writing room purple, Rob built a studio out back, and Max planted pumpkins. Our new border collie cross slept in the front yard, on the same spot favored by the previous owner's black-and-white dog, and Rob and I stood in our yard and made plans together.

Over a year passed before we summoned the courage to go to the mountains again. We steeled ourselves as we topped the rise into Park County, that invisible line we called the Arctic Zone, a snow line well into June. Our little shack-toe sat on the old railroad bed, the screen of aspen trees behind it, the row of pines we planted blocking an unfamiliar truck and a strange white dog, my trails up the hillside invisible from the idling car. It was so familiar yet so distant.

Then I heard a snort and saw the horses—the brown mare and her golden colt, now grown. They stood at the fence, solid and strong in the grass-stickered snow, ears up.

Laura's journal entry for the first day of their three-day tour of Yellowstone Park begins, "Saw the following terraces; Devils' Kitchen, Bunsen Peak, Golden Gate, Rustic Falls, Electric Peak, Apollinaris Spring, Obsidian Cliff, . . ." The sentence ends with a comma and a blank space, as if to be filled in later, but the entry continues: "Built a red hot fire to scare ourselves with. Bess, Christy, and [Martha] had a good time with a certain ranger." The next morning she added, "We were scared by bears, and enjoyed a series of real quakes, [Marie and I] doing the quaking. Before we left we had pictures of a big bear and two little cubs." Her description of Yellowstone ends with, "Today we saw" and another large blank space, followed by, "We went to a dance but did not enjoy it very much. Two men asked me to dance! Eggs! We were all uncomfortable as we wore knickers."

Of Yellowstone Zelma wrote, "We camped at Mammoth Hot Spring Aug. 6 where we collected our mail and got money. We had crossed into Wyoming. For the next three days we made the grand circle trip around Yellowstone Park. We took pictures of Old Faithful and the falls in Yellowstone Canyon. [Had] an encounter with a mother bear and her two cubs at breakfast time. They wanted the syrup on our pancakes. [The rangers scared them off.] We picked up a sample of obsidian (not allowed any more) just as we had treasured a sample of copper in Montana."

Though little was written of what they saw in the park, in interview Laura remembered "the falls. Beautiful. [And] the bears, sneaking around our car at night."

"They huffed and puffed going around the tent," Marie added. "Laura and I were up inside the car, we felt safe," while the others had only canvas to protect them. Then the bears started poking at the cupboard, tugging on it.

By then "I think my teeth were chattering, I was so scared," Laura continued. Grace remembered, "Bears right around us! It was quite an experience seeing a bear, let alone it coming up to our tent!"

After Yellowstone they returned to Bozeman for a rodeo, which they pronounced "ro-day-o." "We left Yellowstone via Gardiner (N) entrance, thru Livingston." Zelma wrote, "We were kicked out of a R.R. park and missed a detour and 'carried the rag' for miles. We ate in a hay field. The car shimmied into Bozeman at 4 p.m. A cross park keeper condescended to let us use the laundry." The campground was on the edge of town, in the lee of a short, steep ridge called Sunset Hills. After cleaning up, they walked to town and the rodeo.

"We thought it would be great to get in on the roundup," Marie remembered. "I was all excited about that. I remember there were tipis around and there were cowboys and calf roping, the whole thing." Zelma wrote, "There was a band concert in the street. We saw bad, rough western characters [and] Indian children. Agnes and Grace danced with the floor manager while Chris and I felt unnecessary. [Martha] out all night again."

Laura's journal reads:

August 9

We saw a real western parade at 11:00 and after lunch we went to the Roundup and had the time of our lives. One man was so badly injured when thrown from a bucking steer (stepped on) that he had to be carried from the field. We saw wild horse riding, bucking horses, bucking steers with a bell under their bellies to make them wild. A huge Brahman bull was brought out, and the news spread that it was the animal that killed a man the day before; another had been gored through the calf of his leg by a mad steer. The steers were big, ugly, long horned, lean creatures and seemed very fierce; anyhow, the cowboys made a point of avoiding them, and they rushed at horses and men on foot.

In the evening Marie, Christie and I went to the movies while the rest of the birds went to a dance. They came home before us!!

I sit on the hill across from my house in Bozeman, Montana. Called Peet's Hill now, it used to be the Sunset Hills, bordering the Sunset Cemetery where the town's namesake is buried and rising abruptly from the lowlands of east Bozeman. Indians camped on this spot and hunted in the tangle of creeks below, now my back yard. Today the unkempt hill is a much loved community open space resembling the golden, rolling sage pasture it used to be, with walkers, joggers, and bikers on the old cow trails.

From the point I can see my chickens, the cottonwoods along the creek, and the whole valley beyond; construction on East Main, the Montana State field house dome, sprawling subdivisions, and the mountain ranges encircling it all: the Gallatins, Bridgers, Spanish Peaks, and Tobacco Roots. Two blocks north of me, below the hill and across the road, is Bogert Park. Enormous ash trees border the wide lawn, the amphitheater, swimming pool, slides, and swings. Originally this was the auto park on the outskirts of Bozeman where the eight women camped almost eighty years ago.

I imagine Laura up early, crawling out of the car to see the same sky I see. Though she's slept only a couple of hours, it's already gathering glow, and the cool, thin air seems charged. She follows a narrow, well-traveled path that leads across railroad tracks and cuts steeply upward. Even this early in the morning the grass is dry—no dew here. That would have worried her father. She wonders how the drought is affecting his crops way back in Iowa. It is such a different land here, fertile and parched at the same time, with great rivers like the Yellowstone rushing all that water past.

At the top of the hill Laura can see across the wide, shadowed valley. She knows that mountains rim it in the distance, but she can't make them out in the dim light. The sun hides behind the cliff-lined canyon they wobbled through the day before, but in the distance it looks like a single, impassable ridge. I wonder, after eight weeks on the road, How does she feel?

Then the sun bursts out, a sudden warmth illuminating everything from the tiny stones underfoot to all those mountain ranges in the distance. Laura sees activity in the camp and heads back for breakfast. I brush off sand and dry grass and head down too. In the rising scent of dust and sage I imagine Laura's feet falling on the same path I walk. Her stride is easy and strong. As our paths cross I feel the rhythm of her breathing.

My great-aunt Laura had nisses in her trees—the tiny tricksters of Norwegian folklore. She put them there on purpose.

She supported herself for years, after her husband's stroke, by painting trunks and commemorative plates with the Norwegian folk art called rosemaling and by making impish, elfish nisses of her own design. Brightly colored, with red jackets and long white beards, they peeped from among the leaves of the enormous oaks framing Laura's home. In a

Galloping Bare-Breasted

neighborhood of old white three-story houses, hers was easy to find.

Myth has it that nisses might occasionally clean your kitchen during the night, but generally they are known as mischievous troublemakers. Laura filled her front room with them, her careful brushstrokes giving each one a unique personality. They waved from the window, slept in the corner, held cats resembling Laura's own, and offered signs reading "Velkommen" (Welcome), "Mange Tak" (Many thanks) and "Putt den i ore dit" (Stick it in your ear).

Whenever Rob and I went to Iowa, an afternoon and evening with Aunt Laura was a highlight of the trip. Supper was pizza, Pepsi, and Snickers bars while watching *Wheel of Fortune*. Only with Laura could that be a celebration. She sat with her cats on her blanket-covered couch under the window, facing us, the TV, and the doorway to the front room. If she heard the little bell on the outer door she called "Coming" in her deep, resonant voice and shooed the cats from her lap to greet the customer or friend.

Her motto was "So what, who cares?" She told me, "You can say that about most things. Not everything. But most things we get upset about in our lives aren't important."

She told us about her Fat Club, a group of ladies who met each week and discussed how to lose weight over doughnuts and coffee. "I'm the only one who ever did lose weight," she said. "And I'll tell you my secret. Carbon mo-noxide."

After Laura had her house insulated she almost immediately fell ill. Her Doctor couldn't diagnose her headaches and nausea until finally it was discovered that her furnace was leaking carbon monoxide into the house. "Before the insulation it just all leaked out," Laura laughed. "But now I always recommend carbon mo-noxide to lose weight."

During and after the Depression she taught school in Phoenix, Arizona. All the single teachers lived in a boardinghouse right in the middle of town. "Oh, we had fun," she said. But like the mythical bird it was named for, Phoenix was born in heat. Sometimes Laura and a girlfriend took canteens and rode horseback into the desert. At sunset the parched landscape wicked golden light and emitted a cool sigh, and Laura and her friend threw off their blouses and urged their horses to a run. Bare-breasted, arms flung wide, they galloped the edge of twilight.

Laura loved to hear about our lives in the mountains of Montana. Perhaps it reminded her of the cabin she had in the Boundary Waters of northern Minnesota after she married, moved back to Iowa, and had two children.

We told her about our plans for our little house, what was accomplished and what was next, and about our adventures skiing and hiking the land around us. Once a wild mother moose charged down the trail toward our old blind, deaf dog. At the last second, the dog leaped into the flashing, striking hooves to land unscathed underneath the moose, which stood with a nearsighted, dumbfounded expression as if to say, "Where did it go?" I hid three feet away behind a thin lodgepole pine.

"Oh, you do a heap of living out there in Montana." Laura exclaimed. "A heap of living."

Though her son had taken over the bulk of the work, Laura continued painting well into her eighties, even as her eyesight dimmed. She painted until she could barely see and the memory in her fingers took over, the images seeming to come directly from her flesh. "I just look forward to it every day," she said, "I love coming down and putting faces on my little nisses."

I asked if she would paint me something with So What, Who Cares on it, and the plate she gave me is my favorite of all her pieces. She couldn't see well enough to stay within her own pencil lines or to erase the pencil afterward, and everything is slightly off center. The nisse in the middle has bright red, slightly overlarge smudged cheeks, but it practically leaps into your lap with arms thrown high and an enormous grin. Around the plate edges her skewed but otherwise perfect lettering declares, So What, Who Cares!

We visited Laura after her first mastectomy. She sat in her usual spot with her usual cats, one named Pusslemot, which she said meant "large orange cat with expressive face," and one called Little Sister. The Torgrim Cat, a barn cat by birth, lurked nearby. She also had a new stuffed bear. "A friend gave me this while I was in the hospital," she said, squeezing it against her cheek. "I was scared in there at night, all alone. But teddy here helped with that."

We didn't stay long, since Laura tired quickly, her sightless eyes becoming sunken and lost-looking despite her resounding voice. We said our good-byes and she stretched out under a soft blanket, her stuffed bear cradled like a child and Pusslemot curled into the hollow of her absent breast.

Yellowstone and the roundup were the last sights they planned to see, though Marie and Laura had four brothers they wanted to visit on the way back to Iowa. They started east again after breakfast. "From [Bozeman] we go to Rapelje and then on to Mercer (if I can get them to go—Gee!)" Laura wrote in her journal. Herman, who worked on an oil rig outside Billings, was their destination that day. "On to Herman's place!" Laura continued, not mentioning that they had run out of money and hoped to borrow some from him. "Herman [had a job], and he had money," Marie remembered. "We didn't think twice about giving money to each other in the family. That's how all of us girls went to college. One or two would work and earn money to help whoever needed it, and when we graduated we were able to help out more."

"At Livingston," Laura continued, "we saw for the first time a man and his mother who helped us twice on the road. If they hadn't been there we'd have been out of luck." Zelma described the day: "Ate lunch at a jail in Big Timber. Saw nasturtiums in bloom. The other car bought a new tire."

"We turned off on a cow path to go to an oil well," Zelma wrote. "Find out Herman had typhoid in the hospital." They toured the camp and oil well quickly and bought butter, but it was still late when they left. They had not planned to drive any farther that day. Zelma noted, "Hump back road to Billings. My first drive at night." Whenever she slowed down to see better, the headlights dimmed.

"After a 35 mile ride," Laura noted, "we went to the St. Vincent Hospital and saw Herman, who seemed very low. We came into camp at about 9:30, and after pitching our tent in a draped effect we finally got to sleep." Zelma added, "The other car goes to the hospital while we go to camp. Supper at 10 p.m. Dishes washed by 11 p.m."

The next morning Laura wrote, "We went up to Hospital to see Herman, and he seemed much better than the night before. The Sisters impressed us as being very nice." Marie remembered, "The nurse who was taking care of him just eyed all of these women coming to see Herman, because she had her eye on him herself. Herman didn't know what was going on; he was sick and I don't think he'd ever even had a date. I always contended that the only way a girl could catch

Galloping Bare-Breasted

him would be with him flat on his back. Well, that's what happened. Of course that [nurse] was Ilene; they were married [over fifty years]."

Herman wrote them a check so they could get home, and on their way out of town Marie sent him flowers.

౿

When Grandma Marie was dying, I bought a candle in a bright blue-and-purple holder, lit it, and waited.

I remembered going with her to visit Grandpa's grave, following her through the graveyard to where new sod was already taking hold. Willard Torgrim, Emma Torgrim, Joanne Torgrim—husband, wife, daughter. It was weird seeing both my names, Emma Joanne, on gravestones next to each other. "This is where I'll go," said Grandma Marie, Willard's second wife. "I won't take up so much space, though. They'll cremate me and put me in a little box right here." Her telling wasn't heavy or morbid, just the last of Grandma Marie's tidy plans.

The Pioneer Graveyard on the edge of Iowa's Washington Prairie is a small, tended plot on an unmarked gravel road among vast fields of corn. Half the graveyard is marked with headstones, and half is smooth, bare lawn dominated by a single stone monument. All the names of those buried long ago under wooden crosses are carved into the ten-foot-high stone. On the east side you can read them; Jacobsen, Thorgrimsen, Olafsen. On the northwest side, despite the pine windbreak, the rock is polished almost smooth. All that remain are shallow wormholes you can feel with your fingertips.

When Grandma Marie took me there she was still herself, with her square gray hair and square hips and skirt—still the stout presence I crashed into, running through the kitchen as a child. As I picked myself up from the floor she smiled and said, "An irrepressible force meets an immovable object."

After Grandpa died, she lived alone for almost twenty years on the small farm on the edge of town. As her stature shrank and her gray hair faded to white, birthdays became important landmarks. "I never had a birthday [party] as a child," she told me when I was ten. "I was born two days after Christmas, and we didn't have much money. My birthday just got lost in the holidays. But when I turned ten, I had a party. My mother said I was a decade old, and that was important. Today you are a decade old." As she got up into her eighties, birthdays became occasions, touchstones to help her count the time. She wanted to live to be a hundred. "One hundred years," she said; "that's enough. Then I can die."

Once she took me to a nursing home. We visited a woman named Anna who was a hundred years old. She had a letter from the president congratulating her. Her response was, "Why is God punishing me this way? Why must I continue living when everyone else is gone?" I didn't understand why we had to sit with her until later when Grandma Marie told me, "She was my teacher. She's the one who convinced me to go to high school. Without her I never would have left the farm."

When Grandma Marie turned ninety, my cousins Greg and Carol threw a huge party. Over a hundred people came. There was a wedding-sized cake with bright flowers on it, and the Luren Singers serenaded her. "I sat like a queen on my throne," she said, describing the receiving line, "And as all those people passed, Carla stood right at my side. It was her job to take care of me that day." Carla was Grandma Marie's five-year-old great-granddaughter.

Though Grandma Marie never bore children of her own,

after forty-five years of teaching her connection with children was quick and telling, her impression lasting. "Always compliment their shoes," she said, "then they'll warm up to you." She had a large extended family, with generations of descendants of her nine siblings, but Carla and her brother Josh were special. Grandma Marie's eyes held a special sparkle when she spoke of them. "They're a little bit of mine, you know," she said.

Grandma Marie began regular babysitting when Carla was six weeks old and her parents, Greg and Carol, went to night school. "I didn't know what to do with a baby so small," she said. "The first night I invited one of the old farm wives from church over; I knew I'd just be lost." Grandma Marie learned how to hold her, how to change diapers, and what her cries meant. As time went on Carla and Josh stayed at Grandma Marie's at least once a week while their parents ran errands or bought groceries in town. They slept in bed with her on special weekend nights. "I told them they can stand on a chair at my house," she once said. "Don't tell their mother." As Grandma Marie got into her nineties and stopped driving ("That's a little bit of dying, you know"), it became the children watching Grandma Marie.

Her mind got fuzzy. She began to forget how old she was. How could she keep track of all those years, and after ninety-five of them—what was one or two anyway? She began to say she was older than she was, and we joked that she would reach a hundred one way or another. Then she began inviting people to her birthday. As they milled around after church, Grandma Marie went from person to person. "My birthday is next week," she said. "I'll be one hundred, you know." Carla corrected her. "No, Grandma. It's in December, and you'll be ninety-six." Grandma Marie nodded, seeming to understand, then the next person would shake her hand and she'd lean over her cane, almost conspiratorily: "My birthday is next week. I'll be one hundred, you know."

Two days after she turned ninety-six, she developed congestive heart failure and nearly died. We rushed her to the hospital and then seventy miles by ambulance to the Mayo Clinic in Rochester, Minnesota, where they saved her. What else can you do? We kept her alive, but Grandma Marie wasn't really there anymore. She didn't recognize anyone and seemed too confused to smile. When at last she was moved from the hospital to the nursing home, she slipped out of her room and wandered around looking for something—home, we guessed. One night she crept into a man's room and tried to crawl into bed with him. He told her she could stay, but she had to sleep on the floor. That's where they found her in the morning. "She's a troublemaker," the nurses said, and they tied her into a wheelchair to keep her from wandering. She soon lost the ability to walk, and then they tied her in to keep her from falling on the floor.

Her ninety-seventh birthday passed uncomprehended. Then she was moved to a different home. The aides set her in the sun next to Beatta, another blind ninety-seven-year-old woman who crocheted and talked to herself. In the way of polite, senile women, they struck up a conversation and soon discovered they'd attended grade school together. "Beatta?" Grandma Marie said, her vague, wet eyes blinking. For days and weeks they sat together, Beatta crocheting a bright quilt she couldn't see and Grandma Marie strapped into her wheel chair. They talked about the one-room school at the end of the maple-lined lane, about the teacher, Anna, who walked five miles to work each day—and how she always followed the railroad tracks because it was the only way clear in winter. They remembered the wood stove in the middle of the schoolhouse and the time they stood too close and scorched their new winter coats. The white heads bobbed with thin laughter as they remembered playmates and pranks ninety years old.

Winter turned to spring and then early summer. One day Grandma Marie looked at Carla and said, "I like your shoes." On his birthday, she told Josh, "You're a decade old now." Everyone was excited at her improvement. She was returning to us. She began to recognize family members, and her gentle humor reappeared. Then she stopped eating. The doctors could find nothing really wrong with her other than very old age, but one by one her systems shut down. Had she remembered that she wanted to die?

I watched my candle's wick flicker on the melting wax and wondered about people dousing themselves in their own essences. I don't know how or why, but I called my cousin Greg the moment she died. Then I blew out the candle. I meant to bury it with her, but I forgot to bring it and watched as that little box went into the ground right where she'd pointed. I forgot to bury it at home in Montana, too, and the next thing I knew the ground was frozen. The candle stub in its bright holder became a part of the array of rocks, jewelry, broken children's toys, and change on my dresser. After a while I didn't think about burying it anymore.

Then one icy winter morning I realized, "Today is Grandma's birthday, she would have been one hundred today." A decade, a century—somehow it had to be celebrated. I dusted the flake of candle and lit it in its holder, watching the flame flicker as it touched the melting wax pool. I thought the short wick might last two hours.

At 6:30 the next morning our smoke alarm went off. The candle was gone, and the kitchen was filled with black smoke as the candle holder flamed into a charred black blob. When the ground thawed I buried it under the lilac hedge, between Tiger the cat and Shooting Star the fish. It didn't take much space.

჻

Billings, Mont.
Aug. 11, 24 8:30 am

Dear Folks:

We are waiting for Grace and Agnes to get back from the P.O. so will start a note home. We are going up to see Herman as soon as they arrive on the scene. Imagine how shocked we were when we came to the oil well and heard that Herman was in the Hospital at Billings—down with typhoid fever. It was time to camp then, but we came the 35 mi. farther on to Billings and found the hospital by 9:00. He was pretty sick. It was quite an effort for him to talk. He said it was hard telling how long he'd have to stay there—might be 2–4 weeks. He's going home to convalesce as soon as he can make the trip. [Handwriting change]

Well, we saw Herman again and he looked pretty good. The nurse told us that Herman would be and is improving this week. We surely were glad to see him and are going on now.

Laura & Marie

Meanwhile Zelma wrote, "We drove around Billings [while] the others got money and went to the hospital."

Then they headed for North Dakota. Laura noted, "On our

Galloping Bare-Breasted

way to Miles City we ran out of gas in the middle of a hill, and a couple of Montana fellows helped us out. Farther on the way we passed them, and when they caught up to us they fired their revolver in fun and we thought we had a blow-out."

The entry continues in a masculine hand, "At Miles City I got this [signature]: Eugene Morgan, Chattanooga, Tenn." Laura's next entry begins with the exclamation, "Good Morning!" and a picture of a heart with an arrow through it. "While the kids were making supper," she wrote, "two eggs chatted continually with them, and while we were eating one of them came over to see if we really ate all the spuds we pre-pared—and we did." Of Miles City Zelma wrote, "We broke back window. Poison oak."

The next day they planned to reach Dickinson, North Da-kota. In the morning they checked their batteries, gas, oil, and air. Zelma wrote, "Hills and valleys for 50 miles; 100 miles of gravel. Swell R.R. station at Glendive. Now we cross into the Black Hills of North Dakota. We have black berries on bread. We see woman with big straw hat from Cal. who always toots twice. 50 miles on red gravel. Chris loses her sun shade. Stall on hill. Mad, bad, hassle. [Then] 14 miles of winding road to Dickinson, the other car not [there.] We camped, danced, set time ahead."

"I slept most of the way to Glendive," Laura noted. "After dinner [noon] we got off the *main* 'Red Trail' and onto the *old* 'Red Trail' We passed through the 'Bad Lands.' [At Dick-inson] Marie tried to buy some milk at a pool hall, hotel, restaurant, and a wholesale house. It was *very* amusing. We camped at the Fair grounds, and after we had gone to bed a fool dance orchestra started so we kids couldn't sleep. 'Agony orchestra.'"

The following morning Zelma wrote, "It was cold to crawl out. Start at 6:15. Wrap up in blankets." It was her last journal entry of the trip, and it ended with, "We leave the other kids for three days." The girls in Ophelia were not interested in visiting Hjelle brothers in Mercer and Portland, North Dakota, so they planned to reunite in Moorehead, Minnesota, in three days. Laura wrote, "On to Mercer—nothing else counts!"

Both Ole and Ben and their families lived in Mercer. Ole ran a bank, and Ben was the postmaster.

Marie too had lived in Mercer. After she taught at her country school for a couple of years, her brother Ole offered her a job at the town school there. She taught the upper grades, but the other teachers had their teaching certificates, and Marie found they just knew more about what to do. By the end of the year she said she "felt like a failure" and was headed for teachers college in Cedar Falls.

But there were two other things she generally said about her time there. She always said she had more fun in Mercer, North Dakota, than at any other time in her life. She remembered a fellow was interested in one of the other teachers. He found an escort for Marie, and the foursome attended every dance within forty miles, sometimes even a hundred miles. Unless the weather was bad.

That was her other vivid memory, of the snowstorms that came sweeping in from the north. People there could see them coming. She never figured out how, but they'd come early for their children and then a blizzard would blow in. One day Marie was the last to leave the school, and when she got to her brother's house the wind held the front door shut. Even with Marie pulling and Cora pushing from inside, it wouldn't budge. Marie had to go around back and climb in the window.

In 1924 the morning chill and endless arid distances were familiar. I imagine Marie's resolve was familiar too; only this time it was Laura she wanted to go to college.

Laura's journal reads:

August 13

We stayed at Ben's for supper and went up to Ole's afterwards. Saw Ella, Ole, Ben, Brandt, Eunice, Margie Anne, Bruce, Cora, Minnie Carlson, and Walter. Also met Jennie Nielson, Anton Hedahl, Minnie Carlson and Freda "something."

August 14

Up quite late. I had a sponge [bath] and dolled up (?) in my white sleeveless sweater and white waist, also other sundries. Went to Turtle Lake in morning with Grace, Ole driving. Managed to get back to Mercer in time for dinner at Ben's. After dinner we draped ourselves around until about 2:00, then visited Ben at Post Office. Later Agnes and I had charge of the Bank. Our main job was enjoying ourselves, Brandt [nephew] assisting us. "Yas . . . No, he ain't in. It's only Auntie Laura and me and Agnes here. . . . Yah . . . Goodbye." In the evening we went out to Brush Lake and were eaten up by mosquitoes but enjoyed ourselves immensely despite it.

August 15

Left Mercer at 7:15 and were all sorry to go. Nothing unusual happened this day until we got to Portland, where we met Carl and Tess. Grace and Agnes slept in a real bed [there] while Marie and I slept on the kids' cots on the porch. We were rather cold.

Grace remembered their stop in Portland, North Dakota, as a high point in the trip. "We had one sumptuous feed at [Carl] the doctor's," she said. "One thing they served, and I still remember it every time the vegetables are ripe and in good shape. I think of the cucumbers and sour cream they served us."

Laura noted, "We got up really early and got an early start, as Tess helped us an awful lot."

~

Besides the Model T journey, Laura and Marie took several other trips together when they were young. "Marie just had a yen, she wanted to see things, and she took me along," Laura said.

If it wasn't for Marie, I would never have gone to Norway, or Europe, or to college. For many years I felt my life would never have amounted to anything without her influence, and I didn't like feeling that way. So one day I sent her a letter. In it I thanked her for everything she'd done for me, for all the opportunities she'd offered, but I also said the things I did for myself. Going to Arizona was my own idea, and so was painting—my rosemaling and the nisses that I love so much. Writing that letter made it all right again. But here I was, eighty years old and still bothered by some of these things. It just goes to show what a big impact one person can have on another.

But her story didn't end there. Her eyes took on a twinkle as she continued:

> Marie still did much more traveling than I did. She was determined. But I remember at the time she was going to Egypt, she was worried because some of the neighbor ladies were talking about how far away it was and that she'd be gone so long. It was in Africa, after all, and she'd be in a primitive area for a whole year. Marie was really worried. So I said to her, "Marie," I said. "Don't listen to those bats. They've never been across the road."

During Laura's sightless years, when neither she nor Marie could drive anymore, the sisters talked on the telephone every day. It was one of their greatest pleasures. Sometimes they just checked in, other times they spent hours reminiscing. They were the last two from their big family.

Marie remembered waking up one day when she was six years old to find her father sitting in the kitchen in his Sunday clothes, all dressed up for breakfast. Usually he wore overalls and was out doing chores by now, but on this morning he just sat in the kitchen, wearing his town hat, church shoes, and everything. Marie knew there was a woman there to see her mother, but she didn't know why.

"Of course back then they always had a midwife at a birth; they never had a doctor to bring in a baby," Marie remembered. "My father was dressed up because he had been to get that midwife to help my mother with her labor."

Marie ate her toast and took Albert and Emma out to play, all the time wondering, "What's going on here? What's the deal?" A short while later they heard a rapping on the window. "We were playing just outside, and when we looked up there was my dad with a new baby. We were just big-eyed. Of course, that baby was Laura."

When Laura was ninety she fell and broke her hip. After three weeks in the hospital, she and her worn teddy bear moved into the nursing home where Marie already lived. For a week the two sisters were in the same home, but in separate wings. Laura couldn't leave her bed, and Marie wandered lost. When Laura died, no one could find her cherished teddy. But it wasn't gone. Somehow Marie had it.

8. A Heap of Living

When Grandma Marie's kitchen table arrived, I realized I'd never before seen it uncovered. The red-and-white-checked tablecloth had always protected it. Now suddenly here it was in my home. My inheritance: round oak, balanced on a central post supported by large curved toes, sagging around the edges as if elbows still rested there and slightly tipped toward Grandma Marie, playing solitaire into the night.

She hates to be idle, but at ninety-five she can't do much else. The black telephone and antique radio sit on shelves in the corner behind her. A small lamp, the only light in the room, rests on the table, pointed right over her playing cards. A wind-up clock ticks at the edge of the spotlight, and yellow sticky notes she's written to herself are stuck to the tablecloth, fanning out into shadow. "Wind clock," "Call Billy," "Wind clock," "Call Billy," all around her. Just out of the halo of light, her cat sleeps in a cardboard box, paws curled under her chest. And I am there too, somewhere in that dark room.

∽

The trip sputtered out like an old Model T. No more letters, and only Laura continued her journal through to the end.

The cars reunited in Minnesota, and the next day Laura wrote that Ophelia was "bumped by an egg in an enclosed car. [It was] an agonizing scene. Their cupboard was torn off and both fenders were bent. Poor kids!" The closer they got to home, the worse the roads became. After two months of arid western roads, gumbo reappeared. Laura wrote, "At Rochester it began to rain and the roads got worse and worse. Near Preston we saw a car drive quietly and gracefully into the ditch. Got as far as [we could] without chains and camped 20 miles from home! Wotta life!"

The next day she wrote, "Chains." The roads were very bad, the worst they'd seen since leaving the state. "That was our welcome home," Marie remembered in an interview: "getting stuck in the mud." Laughing with her, Laura agreed: "Only ten miles from home!"

There is a point in every Montana winter when I begin searching for summer. I drive out west of Bozeman, only an hour or so, to where there isn't any snow and sunshine is already warming the earth. I drive through Pony, Harrison, and Three Forks (which Laura described as "a punk camp with rotten accommodations; free, however"), past the buffalo jump and fields where newborn calves bask on lines of hay and the babysitter cow shakes her shaggy black head at me. Geese fly in Vs and drop onto green-fringed fields, waddling and honking with strange enormity. But the warmth and sun aren't enough. I drive and drive.

Eating pie in Willow Creek, I suddenly realize that for me the season of summer and the season of Iowa are inextricable. Just now my emotional climate matches the cold and darkness of early spring in the northern Rockies. I haven't a creative thought. I want to find that season of Iowa—an endless summer where living is shared and stories and love bubble forth as from a bottomless, steaming trout spring.

I used to stand on Trail Creek, at an elbow in its tangled flow. In winter the ice shards mounted there, a thousand frozen cowlicks pointing upstream. In spring I watched the water flow toward me, then bank and veer away in a rock-clattering sparkle right at my feet. Toward and away at once—it made me dizzy.

Now I drive to the Missouri headwaters, where the Madison, Gallatin, and Jefferson rivers come together. All big rivers, these three merge and flow toward the Dakotas. I stand on the point of dry land at the tumultuous joining. Here my friend saw her toddler fall, disappearing soundlessly into spring runoff. She raced to the spot, torrents of water and ice pounding in her ears, to find him bobbing, clinging desperately to last summer's long grasses—not lost after all.

Seventy miles east, small change in terms of Montana distances, the Yellowstone River also flows. Born in the calderas of Yellowstone Park and fed by many Trail Creeks, it pours from the lake, a big-volume river right from the start, and flows for nearly seven hundred miles before joining the Missouri in western North Dakota.

Divided from each other by a crooked ridge of higher ground, both rivers wind for hundreds of miles through the same arid, golden country before meeting, coalescing, and carving their way toward Iowa.

Our lives weave together like pounding river water. I try to write about my grandmother only, but the connections are too strong. My own stories slip in, along with those of her sister, her mother, and my mother. I can't tease one free, or write about one of us without another. Memories, stories, people, and seasons dissolve, and I am surrounded by water. I stand on a point of dry land while the future boils past me, past Iowa, to where other women pull other children to safety, toward life.

Still, I prefer Laura's metaphor. She claimed she did a heap of living and acknowledged my stories the same way. Perhaps it's because a heap is less orderly than a river flow, or because the human heart sometimes swims upstream. In Iowa the kittens, piglets, and puppies sleep in a soft heap, the pile rising and falling unevenly with all the breathing, but their heartbeats in rhythm. In that heap of life, that summer-colored, milky combination I call "Iowa," my breath is mine but my pulse is ours.

I drive home over dirt roads in the darkness and wind, my single headlight vanishing over washboard ripples. No city glow dulls the night sky, but fast-moving clouds bury it. Beyond them I hear invisible geese honking and catch glimpses of stars and geese flying.

∿

Laura and Marie returned to gray skies and gumbo, the home they left nine weeks and 9,142 miles before. Laura's last journal entry reads, "Started for home and got there at about 10:00. Saw the girls [in Ophelia] for the last time in Decorah."

The scene is the same: the spring creek, the Brick House, the bluffs. The Ford is parked by the woodshed, but now the windshield is covered with stickers and the side curtains with mud, and the Brick House seems smaller. They are still alive.

Then their mother rushes out of the house and engulfs them. After coffee, they unload their car, hang the mud-splattered tent up to dry, and take their suitcase upstairs to their room. As Laura sits on the bed, she feels suddenly confined. The windows draw her to the green outside and the muffled sunshine, and Laura realizes she has not been indoors, seriously inside, in over two months. Once at the window, the white cliffs, moist and overgrown, beckon much as the desert did. Marie joins her at the window. They know the best view is from their window, but they head outside anyway, passing their mother at the sink with still more potatoes as the screen door slams behind them.

❧

Whenever I return to Iowa, I too climb the bluffs. It takes only a moment to crest a crooked trail; it doesn't matter which one—they all lead to the top. I cross the level, shaded ridge to where the limestone tip splits away and leap the cleft to bare rock. I smile in recognition of the ever-present vertigo, then close my eyes and will the familiar updraft across my face, the gust of pigeons.

But when I look west across the patchwork of small fields and straight painted fences, I cringe. It's like a life-sized tedious needlepoint. The vistas of the West are now my home view. I take a deep breath just to prove I can and wonder if Laura and Marie did too. Then I return home by the other path. From the base of the cliffs, I pick my tree and run.

In the Women in the West series

When Montana and I Were Young:
A Frontier Childhood
By Margaret Bell
Edited by Mary Clearman Blew

Martha Maxwell, Rocky Mountain
Naturalist
By Maxine Benson

The Enigma Woman:
The Death Sentence of
Nellie May Madison
By Kathleen A. Cairns

Front-Page Women Journalists,
1920–1950
By Kathleen A. Cairns

The Cowboy Girl:
The Life of Caroline Lockhart
By John Clayton

The Art of the Woman:
The Life and Work of Elisabet Ney
By Emily Fourmy Cutrer

Emily: The Diary of a
Hard-Worked Woman
By Emily French
Edited by Janet Lecompte

The Important Things of Life:
Women, Work, and Family
in Sweetwater County, Wyoming,
1880–1929
By Dee Garceau

The Adventures of the Woman
Homesteader: The Life and Letters of
Elinore Pruitt Stewart
By Susanne K. George

Flowers in the Snow: The Life of
Isobel Wylie Hutchison, 1889–1982
By Gwyneth Hoyle

Domesticating the West:
The Re-creation of the Nineteenth-
Century American Middle Class
By Brenda K. Jackson

Engendered Encounters: Feminism and
Pueblo Cultures, 1879–1934
By Margaret D. Jacobs

Riding Pretty: Rodeo Royalty in the
American West
By Renée Laegreid

The Colonel's Lady on the Western
Frontier: The Correspondence of
Alice Kirk Grierson
Edited by Shirley A. Leckie

A Stranger in Her Native Land:
Alice Fletcher and the American Indians
By Joan Mark

So Much to Be Done:
Women Settlers on the Mining and
Ranching Frontier, second edition
Edited by Ruth B. Moynihan, Susan
Armitage, and Christiane Fischer
Dichamp

Women and Nature:
Saving the "Wild" West
By Glenda Riley

The Life of Elaine Goodale Eastman
By Theodore D. Sargent

Moving Out: A Nebraska Woman's Life
By Polly Spence
Edited by Karl Spence Richardson

Eight Women, Two Model Ts, and the
American West
By Joanne Wilke